KATHARINE STEWART was born in 1914, and is now known as the *Grande Dame* of Highland Literature. During the war, she worked for the Admiralty in London. She then moved to Abriachan, near Inverness, where she ran a croft and wrote documentaries for the BBC.

She has written numerous articles for various magazines and penned several books, including *A Croft in the Hills, Crofts and Crofting, A Garden in the Hills, A School in the Hills, The Post in the Hills* and *The Crofting Way*. She was instrumental in setting up the museum at Abriachan. In April 2005 she received the Saltire Society Highland Branch Award for Contribution to the Understanding of Highland Culture, in recognition of her many works.

D1353072

Luath Press Limited

EDINBURGH

www.luath.co.uk

The Story of Loch Ness

KATHARINE STEWART

Luath Press Limited

EDINBURGH

www.luath.co.uk

First published 2005
This edition 2007

ISBN (10): 1-905222-77-7
ISBN (13): 978-1-9-0522277-3

The paper used in this book is recyclable. It is made from low
chlorine pulps produced in a low energy, low emission manner
from renewable forests.

Cover photograph by Rosemary Holt
courtesy www.tinkerbell-images.co.uk

Printed and bound by
Creative Print and Design, Ebbw Vale

Typeset in 10.5 point Sabon

For Hilda, who smiled on it

Acknowledgements

I SHOULD LIKE TO thank most sincerely Professor Smout for writing the foreword to this book. My very real thanks go to Alistair Macleod, Highland Council Genealogist, for his invaluable help in tracing people and events. I should like to thank, also, the staffs of the Reference and Lending departments of Inverness Public Library, of the Archives and of the Museum, who always found the necessary books and papers and maps, with unfailing patience and courtesy.

I am most grateful to Mrs Cameron of Aldourie, who, with her late husband Colonel Cameron, generously shared her knowledge of south Loch Ness-side and to Mr and Mrs Fraser of Borlum and their daughter Anne, who pointed out the places that are home to them. I am also grateful to Christine Matheson for her study of the geology of Loch Ness. My special thanks go to my daughter Hilda for her company on visits to sites, her work with the camera and her skilled scrutiny of the text.

Contents

Foreword

THIS DELIGHTFUL STUDY of Loch Ness is written with deep knowledge and a lifetime of love of one of the most wonderful spots in the Scottish Highlands. Katharine Stewart invites us to a gentle exploration of place and people. Here birds and beasts, trees and flowers mingle with history and legend; natural beauty and the human past are the frame of present life. There is more, much more, to Loch Ness than the monster, though the monster makes its presence felt. It is neither certainly there nor certainly not there, a feeling that anyone can empathise with who has spent even half an hour looking at that immense and ever changing surface of water. Community is certainly there, with a very strong sense of how it has endured enormous strains and changes, the vacillations of medieval feud, the terrors of Jacobite rising and its repression, the trauma of the replacement of cattle husbandry by sheep ranch, the accompanying emigration, the 19th century arrival of industry and the 20th century outburst of tourism. The great leave their marks, from St Columba and his saints, with their wells and stones, to that proto-tourist Dr Johnson and the 'good Sir James', an 18th century improving Grant laird still remembered with affection, which has not always been the fate of his class and time. But the humble even more assuredly leave theirs, in the tumble of stones that used to be their houses and the green spots on the moor that were once their shielings.

We come to appreciate the life and depth of tradition in

their transhumance farming, in the strath in the winter, in the hills with the cows in the summer, an age-old movement that came to an end with the onset of modern sheep farming. We hear of the martial tradition of the people, exemplified in the 20th century by the Lovat Scouts. There is a chapter on Thomas Telford and the construction of the Caledonian Canal, a feat that took transport engineering literally and metaphorically to new levels. We follow the trials and tribulations of the railway mania that here stretched into the 20th century. It overlapped with another unexpected moment when Loch Ness again found itself at the cutting edge of technology, when the monks of the newly established monastery at Fort Augustus for the first time in Britain made use of hydroelectric power to heat and light a home. A few years later in 1895, hydropower was first used at Foyers on an industrial scale, harnessing the mighty falls to smelt aluminium and incidentally sparking the first serious protest against landscape desecration in Scotland.

But time heals much. Foyers, diminished, is still worth seeing, and parts of the industrial development have become holiday homes. Loch Ness may not quite be Elysium: the traffic speeds dangerously on the Fort William to Inverness road, and not all use of the loch is respectfully quiet. Too few people stop to find and feel the stillness, but for those who do, whether in-dweller or visitor, it is worth it. Try that spot near Cherry Island, 'a rocky slope, relatively inaccessible to man and grazing animals', a taste of the primeval forest and a riot of flowers – 'bugle, wood sage, blaeberry, golden rod, wild strawberry'. That sounds to me very like Heaven. This is a lovely book.

T.C. Smout
Historiographer Royal in Scotland

Introduction

IN TELLING THE story of Loch Ness I have tried to put this huge body of water into its setting as part of what Thomas Telford, that great engineer and man of letters, called a 'remarkable valley.'

Over the last 50 or so years the loch has been closely associated in people's minds with the creatures that may inhabit its depths. But what of the other creatures, furred and winged, which have foraged and flown in its woods and its skies? What of the people who have lived and loved, skirmished and wandered along its shores?

Life for them has been precarious and they know it to be so. Storms have arisen from the deepest calm, calls to arms have been instinctively obeyed, long-standing feuds resolved, sometimes in bloodshed, loyalties strained. But the treasures were always there and still are today – leaf-buds on the birches on a morning in May, the cries of the wild swans winging in at an autumn dusk, the scent of the bog myrtle in summer, the wonder of ice crystals on the silent winter burns.

Alexander Macdonald, a descendent of one of the 'Seven Men' of Glen Moriston who sheltered the Prince in the cave of Coire Dho, came from Achnaconeran in the heights over Invermoriston. He was known as *Gleannach*, a 'man of the glen'. In the introduction to a book of folklore, stories and poetry he published in 1914 he said:

Few districts in Scotland can vie with Loch Ness-side for song and story. It is a land of poetry and romance ... where bards sang for generations untold, and where seannachies never wearied of relating tales of the days of old. The author ... is a native of this poetic country, whose privilege it was as a boy to listen with rapturous attention to those stories and songs, amidst scenes and circumstances congenial in many respects.

In a reprint by the Gaelic Society of Inverness which appeared in 1942, many of the poems are translated into English and the music for a number of them is included. 'Words alone without a sense of music behind them, mean so little to the Highlander', as Alexander's daughter, also a writer, said.

Gleannach tells of the lairds and the bards, the pipers and the reivers, the travellers, the craftsmen, the crofters, all the hardy characters who loved life by the loch with its hazards and its joys.

I hope the story in the present book may convey something of the rich life of this great glen.

Katharine Stewart

The Geology of Loch Ness

TO UNDERSTAND THE geology of Loch Ness we must travel back in time, to over 500 million years before Scotland was joined to England. Scotland formed part of a large continent which included North America and Greenland and was known as Laurentia. England and Wales were part of a smaller land mass, Avalonia, which was separated from Laurentia by the Iapetus ocean. As Laurentia, Avalonia and a third continent, Baltica, were drifting towards each other, the Iapetus ocean shrank, until finally, 410 million years ago, the Iapetus ocean closed, uniting Scotland and England.

The impact of the collision of these land masses resulted in the formation of the Caledonian mountains. These mountains were built from sedimentary rocks, which were buried deep within the Earth's crust and were forced up and transformed by heat and pressure to form the Moine schists which now cover most of the central Highlands. Associated with the continental collision was the intrusion of granite magma, which originated from the partial melting of rock from a deeper level within the crust, where the heat and deformation was most intense. The granites forced their way up to higher levels, often along deep-seated faults and pre-existing weaknesses in the crust, and helped to elevate the mountain chain. The Abriachan and Foyers granites were formed between 410 and 390 million years ago. Secondary 'abriachanite' – blue crocidolite, aegerine and haematite – have been deposited along joints in the Abriachan granite. These minerals resulted from chemical alteration of the granite when it was at great depths below the fault zone. Good examples of these minerals can be seen at the outcrop near the Abriachan gardens. The Caledonian mountain range, which took 250 million years to form, was at least the size of the Swiss Alps and possibly even as high as the Himalayas.

The Great Glen Fault was initiated towards the end of the Caledonian mountain building period and has remained a plane of weakness in the Earth's crust. It is one of the most spectacular geological features of Britain. This excellent example of a tear fault fractured across the Moine schists about 400 million years ago. The fault occupies a zone about 0.6 km wide, along which considerable movement has taken place on several occasions during a long span of geological time. Minor tremors associated with the fault are still being recorded. Crushing, fracturing and milling down of rocks along the fault zone have resulted in material which has weathered and eroded more rapidly than the surrounding hard rocks. Although this shattered rock is mostly under Loch Ness, it is also evident in road cuttings by the loch between Lochend and Abriachan, Urquhart Castle and Foyers. During the ice ages, when glaciers filled the valley, rocks caught in the slow moving ice scoured away the valley sides and floor. This process resulted in the formation of a very deep valley with steep hillsides. Loch Ness dates from the end of the last ice age, 10,000 years ago.

Over millions of years the Caledonian mountain range eroded rapidly to form the sediments of the old red sandstone. Meall Fuar-mhonaidh, on the northwest shore above Loch Ness, has some of the highest outcrops of old red sandstone conglomerate in Scotland. Originally formed in the valley basin, this mountain was thrust up by faults associated with the Great Glen Fault. Middle old red sandstone conglomerates are exposed in the countryside between Loch Duntelchaig and Loch Ness. There is an outcrop of middle old red sandstone parallel to the loch on both sides, with very occasional fossil bands on the south side. Towards the south end of Loch Ness, the rocks exposed are granites, pegmatites and gneisses of Moinian age (800–1,000 million years old). Substantial movement took place shortly after the deposition of the old red sandstone sediments. Several faults associated with the Great Glen system can be seen between Inverfarigaig and Foyers, cutting Moinian, middle old red sandstone and the Foyers granite.

Christine Matheson

The Big Loch

IT IS A huge body of water, a live body, lying serenely smooth on a summer day, rearing and cavorting in fantastic movement at a time of winter storm. Statistics state that it is 24 miles long, a mile or so wide, 1,000 feet deep and holding 260,000 million cubic feet of water. But that is only the sum of its parts. Deep as the hills surrounding it are high, fed by little rivers and burns and waterfalls, it is bedded in the fault-line of the Great Glen, caused when the earth's surface cracked, split and moved sideways many millions of years ago. This was a time of mountain building, when the Scottish Highlands may have equalled the Himalayas in scale. Subsequent erosion has reduced their size drastically, ice being the major factor. As the climate warmed, melt water deposited gravel in ridges known as eskers. On one of them stands the wooded hill of Tomnahurich, now forming the picturesque cemetery of Inverness.

The melting also left piles of rock debris, known as moraines, seen at the west end of the loch. Raised beaches can also be seen at Invermoriston and Drumnadrochit, forming land now valued for cultivation.

The bed of the loch is an uneasy bed at times, when the never-ceasing movement at the heart of the planet makes for disturbance. Signals can be read. The water never freezes. In cold weather mist hangs over the surface, mist as thick as smoke, as though the water were on fire. Perhaps a reminder of what is raging below? Between 1768 and 1906 more than 56 quakes were recorded in the Great Glen.

In the book *Beauties of Scotland* by Forsyth, published in 1808, it is stated:

> 1st November 1755: a great earthquake at Lisbon, the water of Loch Ness was agitated in an extraordinary manner. The water rose rapidly and flowed up the lake from east to west with amazing impetuosity. It continued ebbing and flowing for about an hour at the end of which time a wave much greater than the others terminated the commotion, overflowing the north bank of the lake to the extent of three feet.

This Glen is a cleft 60 miles long that cuts diagonally across the heart of northern Scotland. Some 20,000 years ago the melting of the ice smoothed the area and four lochs were created – Lochs Linnhe, Lochy, Oich and Ness – linking the southwest of the country to the northeast, from the Atlantic to the North Sea. The Great Glen is one of the features of the planet visible from outer space. Of the four lochs, Loch Ness is the largest and the one still most closely associated with human life.

People whose days and nights have been spent over generations near the shores have developed a deep respect for the loch. Water, the prime element of life, has always been revered. Wells and springs, with their cleaning and healing properties attributed to god or saint, have been venerated. But a body of water the size of the big loch inspires an element of fear. The aspect is studied daily. Every shape and shadow of hill or cloud conveys meaning – a portent of storm, of needed rain, of calm for a sail.

As a waterway the loch has carried craft of all kinds, from the frail coracles of the early travellers who found sailing easier than forays into the wild dry land, to the power-driven trawlers and pleasure-cruisers of today. Fish have provided sustenance for those skilled and hardy enough to take them. But lochside people have always gone warily, sensing the unpredictable, knowing that the long wind can sweep down this huge gully, the sudden impact causing a fearsome turbulence. The sense of wonder and awe at the play of natural forces, a sense now so largely outgrown, was very real to the former people of the loch.

It was that sense of wonder and awe that inspired the stories, the legends, the myths, and gave a special richness to life. This is a land fit for the Fenians, that band of men from ancient Ireland whose deeds of great daring and chivalry must have inspired many young men in the early years of our era. To qualify as a Fenian, a follower of the legendary hero Finn MacCool, the tests were hard.

No man was taken until he were a prime poet, versed in the twelve books of poetry. No man was taken unless he could ward off nine spears thrown at him all at once. Not a man of them was taken till his hair had been put into plaits and he had run through the woods followed by the others, his start being only the width of one branch... Unless he could, at full speed, jump a stick level with his brow and pass under one level with his knee, and unless he could, without slackening his pace, extract a thorn from his foot, he was not taken into Fiannship.

Below the Red Rock on the north side of the loch and near the cleft known as the Pit of the Giant, there is a cave on Creag nan Uamh (the Rock of the Caves). Outside this cave stands a large stone called Clach nan Fiann (the Rock of the Followers of Finn). This name would seem to indicate that Finn and some of his followers had indeed been in the area.

Much of the heroic quality of former times remains in the area of the big loch. Storm-tossed craft have perished, feuds have been fought out on the water, and there have been tragic drownings. Seismically, things may have quietened over many thousands of years, but still today tremors are felt along the fault-line, tremors strong enough to set the teacups quivering, as on a storm-tossed ship. And there is movement in the rocks. Boulders crash from the rock-faces, though modern man has tried to halt the falls with curtains of steel mesh.

Along the shore, woodland flourished. Juniper was one of the earliest trees to appear after the melting of the ice. Birch, hazel and rowan soon followed, rooted precariously in small rock crevices. Thus provided with food and shelter animals soon found a living – bear, wolf, boar, lynx, fox and deer could roam and prosper among the trees and crags. There was habitat for birds too, woodland birds, birds of the rock faces, water birds. And in the loch were fish – arctic char, pike, eel, trout, as well as the salmon. The animal kingdom along the loch shore, living to its own rhythm, surely had the best of times.

The Early Dwellers

IN NEOLITHIC TIMES, about 4000 BC, when people were beginning to appear, it is not likely that many would have settled in the immediate vicinity of the loch. With rock faces rising sheer from the water in some parts, others being densely wooded and making a habitat for those dangerously wild animals, not easily overcome with the weapons of the time, places suitable for human habitation would have been few, except for the small areas of flat ground at the river estuaries. The uplands to the north and south of the loch were preferred. These show evidence of occupation by early peoples – flint arrowheads, stone implements and other artefacts have been picked up over the years. Bronze and Iron Age occupation is also clear. Hut circles, small walls and clearance heaps are numerous. Duns were built near Foyers and across the water at Bunloit and on the site of the later castle at Urquhart bay; small fortified places for protection and from which signals could be sent to warn of the approach of an enemy, land or waterborne. Hunter-gatherers had become agriculturists, keeping livestock and growing small crops of grain evolved from the wild grasses. When settlement came, with the acquisition of property in land, cattle, crops, enmity followed.

Soon, spiritual leaders, men of superior intellect and ability, who claimed to have powers of divination and healing, emerged and exercised considerable influence over the lives of the settled people. These were the Druids. They venerated trees and would conduct rites and ceremonies in groves of oak. Human sacrifice was sometimes called for but on the whole they worked for the good of communities, acting as teachers as well as prophets and healers. Almost within living memory people in an upland area would still consult the 'Druid' who lived down by the loch about weather prospects for the harvest. Doubtless an old man who still dwelt near the great oak groves, he was given the honorary title that lived on!

One charming, though fanciful, story concerning the name given to the big loch involves a Druid known as Daly. In his time, so the story goes, the whole glen was fertile land, with a healing well blessed by himself and covered with a slab of stone. He had given strict instructions that after water was drawn this cover was always to be replaced. One day, a woman, filling her pail, heard a cry from her child left at home. Was he in danger of falling in the fire? She started at once to run back, forgetting, in her haste, to replace the stone lid. The water rose and overflowed, filling the valley. The people rushed to the hills, shouting in despair – '*Tha loch 'nis ann*' – 'There is a loch there now.' So the name – *loch Nis* (pronounced Neesh).

Another romantic story concerns the Irish girl Deirdre who fled the unwelcome attentions of King Conacher of Ulster with her lover Naois. She gave her name to the fort – Dun Dearduil – where they are said to have lived, happily hunting the deer and spearing the salmon and finding honey from the wild bees. A song of Deirdre's goes thus:

Beloved land, that eastern land
Alba with its lakes.
Oh that I might not depart from it
But I go with Naois,
Glen Urchuain, o Glen Urchuain,
It was the straight glen of the smooth ridges
Not more joyful was a man of his age
Than Naois in Glen Urchuain. [i.e. Glen Urquhart]

Could Naois have given his name to the loch on which they looked out every day? Names certainly linger long after their origins are forgotten. Most historians now consider that the loch was named after the river, a stretch of water about six miles long which runs from the loch to the north sea at the port of Inverness – 'inver', from Gaelic *inbhir*, meaning confluence.

During the early centuries of our era those people living in the river estuaries or in the uplands were the Caledonii. To the Romans in the south they were known as Picti, the painted ones, from their habit of daubing woad on themselves when going into battle. This appellation, originally meant as derogatory, has stayed and we now call them the Picts. They were a hardy, vigorous people, skilled horsemen and sailors and with artistic talents expressed in the working of metal and especially in the sculpting of stone, wonderful examples of which survive today. It is said that the Romans, who did not penetrate their northern fastnesses, tried often to acquire their recipe for heather ale, which, it was thought, made them invincible!

After the departure of the Romans in the 5th century AD and with the progress of Christianity, missionaries began to make their way from the west to the land of the Picts. A difficult journey it was, in small coracles, boats of hide, which had to be carried overland between the lochs of the Great Glen. The names of Erchard in Glen Moriston, Drostan in Glen Urquhart and many others – Donnan, Moluac, Cumine, Curadan – are still remembered. They were all zealous and hardy missionaries, bringing their gifts and knowledge to benefit the people. Gradually, their doctrines of mercy and forgiveness supplanted the more barbarous teachings of the former spiritual leaders, the Druids.

Perhaps the greatest of them was Columba, a robust and vigorous Irishman of noble descent, who had settled, with a company of monks, on the island we now call Iona. In the year 565 he came, with 12 followers, by boat, through the Great Glen, to parley with the Pictish king Brude (or Bridei) at Inverness. So many missionaries came by this watercourse that it became known as the 'Valley of the Saints'. These good men have joined the vanished people now, but their legend lives on. The cross appeared, a clear symbol, on the huge carved monuments made by the Picts to whom they preached. Through succeeding times of terror and distress the message was to linger, sometimes only in whispers, in hidden places in the hills.

The Sunlit Shore

TODAY, LEAVING INVERNESS by the high road to the west, labelled the A82, we come to places we can identify as parts of the early and of the later human settlement.

To the north, beyond the cemetery of Tomnahurich (the hill of the yew trees) said to be one of the most beautiful in Europe, is the hill of Craig Phadrig (Patrick's Crag), where the remains of a huge fort can be seen. It was probably a place of refuge for people in times of trouble. It is said to be where Saint Columba met the Pictish king Brude.

A little further, to the south of the road, at Torvean, now a disused quarry, a massive silver chain, with 33 double circular locks, was discovered by men working on the Caledonian Canal in 1808. Torvean was a place of importance as it commanded a ford across the River Ness. Here, also, at Kilvean (Kil from the Gaelic *cille*, meaning church) was a small church founded by Baithean, a cousin and faithful follower of St Columba. Christian churches were often built on former pagan sites. It was Baithean, according to Adamnan, who wrote the life of the saint, to whom Columba said, as he lay near to death, transcribing the 33rd psalm, 'Let Baithean write the words that follow'. Here, it is said, Gruoch, Macbeth's wife, is buried. She is seen, from time to time, a ghostly figure, washing gaunt hands in the river.

At Bona (Gaelic *ban ath* – white crossing), the narrows where the loch emerges into the river Ness, it is recorded that a Pictish ruler had a fort. This was certainly a strategic point, the ford here part of the track from the north which, in later times, became the drove-way for cattle being taken to markets in the south.

In medieval times a castle was built here, Castle Bona, and it was occupied by opposing clans over the years. After a particularly bloody battle between Macleans and Camerons around 1450 AD, caused mainly by cattle raiding, when prisoners on both sides were murdered, it became known as 'Castle Spiridal', the Castle of Ghosts. It was demolished when it was found to be in the way of the Canal.

From here, along a path to the lighthouse, the loch is first seen in its real splendour, stretching, between its shapely hills, with the curvature of the earth, to the infinity of the sky. Feuds and bloodshed are best forgotten.

Back to the main road and past the group of houses at Lochend there are lay-bys for the tired motorist, cyclist and walker. A seat on the little stone wall, with the small waves breaking on the pebble beach, is a real respite. Here, in summertime, are tiny wild strawberries for the picking. The little white roses shine against the grey boulders. Honeysuckle scrambles up the birches, foxgloves stand tall and the sunlit gorse is a dazzle of gold. There's wild thyme among the turf, the thyme that made drinks and medicine for the people down the ages. An osprey may fly over, questing for fish for its young. They nest not far away. Coltsfoot, which filled a pipe when tobacco was scarce and dear, is an early and welcome flower. In later spring primroses star the moss among the birches. Violets, wood sorrel, wood anemone and tormentil stay half hidden among the springing grass. In winter the bare birch branches make a slender tracery of mauve. Autumn, of course, displays a panoply of gold, red, purple, russet, in the leaves, the heather and the bracken.

At Dochgarroch an ancient burying-ground beside the church contains many interesting old gravestones. This was the site of an early Christian chapel, where St Curadan was missionary. The stone where he rested on his journey up the hill and over to Caiplich to minister to the people can still be seen.

The small primary school at Dochgarroch is well attended. It has all the amenities of any modern school, with the added attraction of wild animal and plant life just over the playground wall. Roe deer poke their heads up before they scamper off. Rabbits, hares, a daring fox – these all appear. Otters are not far off and the osprey flies over on its way to fish. Wild flowers are fiercely protected.

The school has been presented with an Eco-Schools Green Flag, only the second school to have one, for its work in recycling of waste materials, in putting posters on all the lochside wheelie-bins and in clearing the beaches of litter, as well as, of course, for its care of wildlife. In all these activities the parents are willingly involved.

To the right of the road, in extensive and attractive grounds, bright with rhododendrons in spring, stands Dochfour House, home of the Baillie family, now the Lords Burton. The present house, in Italianate style, is comparatively new, the original having being burnt down after the Battle of Culloden in 1746, when the family was accused of sheltering Jacobite supporters and of hoarding grain for their use.

The road along this north side of the loch was engineered from a rough track in the 18th century by Sir James Grant, who had land in nearby Glen Urquhart. His men had difficult and dangerous work to do to make a road 'fit for carriages'. Previously the usual way from Inverness to the west lay along the high ground in Caiplich, which is only a track now, but can still be walked.

In 1297, during the Scottish War of Independence, a battle had taken place on this high ground between Highland patriots and men of the English occupying forces. It is well described in E.M. Barron's *The Scottish Wars of Independence*.

Urquhart Castle played some considerable part in the Scottish Wars of Independence. In May 1297 it was occupied by the English, the Constable being Sir William Fitzwarine. Andrew de Moray, Scottish patriot, planned an attack on Urquhart Castle. This extract deals with the clash that took place in Caiplich:

> Sir Reginald le Chen despatched an appeal to Edward for help, and a little later summoned his subordinates to take counsel with him at Inverness. Thither, accordingly, Sir William Fitzwarine, the Constable of Urquhart Castle, betook himself on the morning of Sunday, 25th May. But Andrew de Moray was well advised of the movements of his foes, and when the English knights were sitting in close conference in the Castle of Inverness, the object of their deliberations was hurrying with his men to prepare a surprise for Fitzwarine.
>
> The conference ended. Fitzwarine got to horse. The times were troubled, so a strong escort rode with him, but he anticipated no danger, least of all from those rogues whose fate he had just been deciding. So by the old hill road which wound over the shoulder of Dunain and thence by way of the Caiplich, where the burgesses of Inverness were wont to cut their peats, he took his way, a rough uneven way no better

than the hill tracks which abound to this day. His escort was strong, well-armed and mounted, and a brave sight they made as they rode along the parlous path, expecting no danger, and discussing, perhaps, the chances of an onfall on the rebels at Avoch before they fled in fear. For how could they hope to stand against the knights and men-at-arms of England? And so, armour clanking, accoutrements jingling, they cantered on.

On a sudden came a slight sound, a faint whir-r-r, a flight of arrows, a rush of armed men. The spot, be sure, was well chosen, for well did Alexander Pilche and the burgesses of Inverness know every turn, every evil brae, every treacherous boggy bit, every likely spot for an ambush, on that weary road. Horses and men went down before the wild onset, the air was full of shouts and cries, the ringing of arms on armour, and the groans of wounded men, in one brief moment the whole aspect of the day was changed, and where before there had been the quiet of a May evening, there was now the noise of battle and a fierce confused melée. For a little it looked as if not a man of all the English force would escape. But they had two great advantages over their foes. They were mounted, and they were clad, in part at least, in armour of proof. And in right good stead did these stand them now, for Fitzwarine and some of his men were able presently to break clear of the melée, and driving their spurs deep into their horses' flanks, gained in safety the shelter of Urquhart Castle. But they left behind them two of Fitzwarine's principal followers, who fell sore wounded into de Moray's hands, and a number of lesser men, whose fate is not recorded. They lost, too, 18 horses, a grievous loss in a country where horses accustomed to carry knights or men-at-arms were difficult to obtain, and they had been compelled to flee before the foe they despised. It was a great day for de Moray and his little army. They had struck a strong blow for freedom, and they had won.

When, in September 1934, the loch road was widened to take the increase in motor traffic along what was known then as 'Glen Albyn', a cave with stalactites and stalagmites, which had for many years sheltered wayfarers and 'travellers', as the tinker people were known, was destroyed. Huge cliffs of rose-red granite line the route and high above – best seen from the other side of the loch – is the 'Pit of the Giant', an enormous cleft in the rock. Up there are many caves. In one, a cattle-raider and outlaw named Cameron took refuge and lived well enough for several years in the 1800s, when the law was threatening him.

A little past the turning sign-posted 'Abriachan' is a small graveyard, its presence indicated by a group of large cypress trees. This is Kilianan – a chapel dedicated to St Finian, an Irish spiritual leader who taught Columba. Here some Columban monks settled after the saint's journey from Iona to Inverness in 565, to parley with King Brude. On the way, reaching a point some ten miles short of their destination, it appears he stopped on this small green shelf, facing the morning sun, with water cascading from the rocks above into deep pools, ideal for drinking and washing. Traces of the monks' small cells can still be seen and a large heart-shaped stone, at a little distance up the hill, is known as Columba's Font Stone. A man-made hole in the centre is always – miraculously it seems, for there is no apparent source – filled with water.

Eona MacNicol, whose family belonged to Abriachan, writing of the Font Stone, says:

> The power attributed to the stone agrees with what is known of St Columba, a special interest in women in childbirth. It was believed up to a generation ago [early 1900s] that the water held in the round hole was of benefit to women in child-

birth. My parents remembered also that infants had a few drops of the water put into their baptismal bowl. There is mystery about the water. It is present even in dry weather and if the hole empties it fills quickly, though there would seem to be no inlet to allow the entry of spring water. Birth and death the forgotten saints preside over; marriage, too, or rather betrothal, which in the old highlands was almost equivalent. A little higher up the hill slope, no doubt part still of the holy ground, its site now known to few, if any, in Abriachan, stands the handfasting stone. This bears hollows capable of accommodating the hand in three different positions.

With hands joined through the stone, and with one witness to the occasion, the couple could consider themselves married for a year and a day. If then they decided to part, they were free to do so. If they chose to stay together they could seek the blessing of the church on their union.

The Columban monks were skilled craftsmen and farmers and would have taught young men the arts of husbandry, the uses of healing herbs and probably the elements of wood and metalwork.

Another skill they brought with them from Iona was that of the illumination of manuscripts. They would also pass on some words and phrases of Latin and Greek to enable the people to take part in their simple forms of worship. They were, in fact, the first educators in the Highlands and this would have been one of the first schools.

Lately, a cross-marked stone has been discovered of a type that indicates Christian occupation of the site into the 8th or 9th centuries. At one time it was thought that the parish church of Bona stood there. In the 18th century it was a 'Preaching Site'. It had certainly long been a sanctuary; the sanctuary stone still stands. Anywhere within a radius of a mile thence was considered a safe refuge from the law. It is thought that some of the Macdonalds from Glencoe sought safety there after the massacre in 1692. Many families of that name subsequently settled in the area.

For long ages and until quite recently burials were made at Kilianan. Mostly the dead lie in quiet, unmarked spots. But one burial of note is very skillfully marked: a finely carved slab, a pair of shears at the foot denoting the burial-place of a woman. This 'recumbent grave-slab' is recorded in the *Proceedings of the Society of Antiquaries*, volume XXXVI. It is said, in local tradition, that it covers the remains of a 'Norwegian Princess'. She could have been the descendant of a Viking family settled in nearby Glen Urquhart, who had been well accepted by the people.

Mr Angus Grant, a local man, noted in 1892,

> This ground is very old and Gaelic scholars aver that its name indicates its having been dedicated to St Columba. There is a tradition that these stones and many others now lost all originally belonged to Kilianan but that, in the absence of any surveillance, they were taken away by anybody who chose to engage in such sacrilege. It is said that a boat loaded with sculptured stones in the course of removal from Kilianan was wrecked on loch Ness and that, within living memory, the stones could be seen, on a clear day, at the bottom of the loch.

In the early year this graveyard is bright with snowdrops, primroses, daffodils and blossoming trees. Later, the bluebells flower, a fitting memorial for a sanctified site. It is also fitting that the hillside is now a nursery garden growing plants of great beauty, which are sent to all parts of the world. The gardeners are keen conservationists and have engineered pathways up the slopes, some edged with dry-stane dykes, with the organically grown plants linked into the natural surroundings of fern and moss. Above the garden are the huge oaks, descendants of those of pagan times.

Up the steep road to the right, just before the graveyard, past the small abandoned quarries of red granite and the rushing waters of the burn is the erstwhile crofting settlement of Abriachan. Here, people of the Stone, Bronze and Iron Ages lived, leaving traces of their occupation in the form of hut circles, flint arrowheads, scrapers and other artefacts. In one place, in the high ground of Caiplich, after a particularly heavy burning of the heather in spring some 40 years ago, a small Bronze/Iron Age village was uncovered, consisting of eleven huts, dividing walls and clearance heaps. A plaque at the roadside identifies it. Until well into the 20th century the land at Abriachan was continuously cultivated, fields being dug out of the encroaching heather, sometimes with the old foot-plough. When the old saying held good – 'A deer from the forest, a fish from the stream, a tree from the wood' – life could be pleasant enough. There was material to hand for the building of houses – walls of stone or turf, rushes or heather for thatch – and there was peat for firing. In later times, when economic necessity, with its rules and regulations, became the order of the day, many people left, or were obliged to leave, to make a living elsewhere. Some, today, come back to look for their origins, seeking that elusive element that their present life lacks.

In more recent times Abriachan became known locally as 'the place that was bombed', after a German airman, anxious to get rid of his load, which had been meant to destroy the aluminium works on the other side of the loch, jettisoned the bombs harmlessly in the heather.

The Second World War made another impact on the area. One stormy night – New Year's Eve, 1940 – a Wellington bomber, on a training flight, crashed into Loch Ness.

The plane later was discovered by monster-hunters taking soundings. It was raised in 1985 and was so well preserved in the peaty silt of the loch floor that, when a battery was inserted into the electric fittings, the lights came on! It has been restored and is now housed in an aircraft museum in England. A plaque at the roadside, recently set up, tells the story.

To return to Kilianan and Columba – his visit to King Brude at Inverness has been well documented by his biographer Adamnan, in his writings a century and a half later. As well as making a favourable impression on the king, the saint also managed partly to overcome the hostility of Broichan, the king's Druid and foster-father. One strange encounter, which might have impressed the most sceptical, was that of one of his followers with a fierce creature in the river, near the king's palace. As the animal's jaws were about to close on the man's head, Columba raised his hand, shouted in his stentorian voice and the creature sank out of sight. What kind of creature was it? Some think it might have been a giant pike or sturgeon. At that time there were many water creatures about – otter, which are still there, beaver, the occasional seal. The local people must have wondered if this man could work miracles. Broichan, of course, was not easily impressed. When Columba was about to make the return journey to Iona the Druid prophesied a devastating storm. Undeterred, the saint and his followers set sail. The wind rose. Skilled sailors as they were, they tacked and veered until it changed, as they foresaw it would, and eventually blew them west.

Strange Creatures in the Loch?

IT IS AT a place near the turning to Abriachan that one of the first documented sightings of a strange creature occurred. On the evening of 5 January 1934 Peter Grant, a young veterinary student, was returning home from Inverness on his motorcycle. It was a dark night. At about 1:00 am, as he approached the Abriachan road-end, the sky cleared, revealing bright moonlight. He noticed a large, dark object on the right-hand side of the road, in the shadow of the bushes. Then a small head was turned towards him and a large animal crossed the road in two bounds and disappeared in the loch, making a huge splash. Grant noted that it had 'a long neck and oval-shaped eyes, with a powerful tail of 5–6 feet'. He reckoned the whole animal measured some 15–20 feet.

The previous year, in May 1933, the newspaper the *Inverness Courier* had received a story from Mr Alexander Campbell, water bailiff at the other end of the loch, of a large aquatic creature. The editor, Dr Evan Barron, said: 'Well, if it is as big as you say it is, then it must be a real monster.' So was born the appellation which has remained with the creature ever since.

People whose families have lived near the loch shore for generations have always been reluctant to talk about the creature in the water. There is a sort of taboo about it. Stories of the 'water-horse', the 'kelpie' as it is known, linger in the memory. Should you seek a ride on the back of this handsome black steed, with one huge gallop he would plunge you into the water and drag you to the black depths.

In 1802, a crofter in Abriachan, Alexander Macdonald, told a friend that he had several times seen an unusual animal in the loch. Once, when he was rescuing a lamb from a precarious position on the crags, the creature swam quite close inshore, before turning and making out into the open loch, then submerging with a great commotion. He reckoned it was about 20 feet long, and he said it reminded him of a salamander. The name stuck. For many years the skipper of the ferry at the beginning of the 20th century, putting into the pier, would shout to the pier-master: 'Seen the salamander today, Sandy?'

Boys and girls from Abriachan would go swimming by the pier, where there is a sheltered pebble beach. The water is cold and dark, but not unwelcoming. One admires those brave enough to swim the breadth and even the length of this vast expanse of water, with all its native inhabitants!

This pier, now ruinous, is one of the many on either side of the loch at which the steamers run by the firm of MacBrayne would call regularly with freight and passengers. The most famous boat, the *Gondolier*, launched in 1866, made the passage until 1940, when she was sunk at Scapa Flow as part of the barricade against German U-boats. On the very day she was broken up her last skipper, Captain John Macdonald, died. In his 40 years' service with the *Gondolier* he reckoned he had sailed the loch many times yet he had never seen any strange creatures there.

An Niseag (pronounced 'neeshack') is the Gaelic name for the so-called 'monster', the diminutive '–ag' ending of the word signifying affection, perhaps propitiation. It is interesting to note that in Blaeu's *Atlas*, published in 1653, it is stated, regarding Loch Lomond, 'Waves without wind, fish without fin and a floating island.' Could there have been a mystery about that loch then, too? Loch Morar, in the west Highlands, the deepest loch in the country, has a resident creature known as 'Morag.' As her loch is remote she is mostly left in peace, though she has been known to cause commotion enough to upset fishermen's boats.

Over the last 70 years or so there have been many reported 'sightings' of a water beast in Loch Ness and many explanations of what may or may not have been seen. Was it a swimming deer, turbulence caused by a tremor from the depths...?

An Niseag keeps her own counsel, surfacing when it pleases her to scent the summer air, retreating to the shelter of the deep underwater caves in winter storms, finding sustenance enough to rear the generations. It could have been one of her ilk, a serpent-like form, depicted on a carved stone of prehistoric date, found at Balmacaan, near the loch.

In 1933, when the 'monster' story first appeared in print, Bertram Mills offered £20,000 for the delivery of the creature alive at the circus. The Chief Constable gave orders to prevent anyone shooting at it or attempting to trap or molest it in any way. Wise man! A cage was actually prepared for shipment to Loch Ness should the animal be captured.

It was at this time, the mid 1930s, that the road along the north side of the loch, Glen Albyn, was being upgraded. The work entailed much blasting of rock, the movement of men and of heavy machinery, disturbances of many kinds. This perhaps accounts for the fact that no more land sightings were recorded in this area. *An Niseag* was keeping her distance. No water sightings were reported by the engineers, but, as the road progressed, more tourists and journalists appeared and stories of the 'monster' were published in the London papers. To people whose main concern was making a somewhat precarious living on the shores of the 'big water', these incursions of men and women loaded with cameras, telescopes, recording instruments, seemed unbelievably ridiculous. Their natural courtesy forbade them to express their incredulity to the people they saw and met. There were creatures in the loch – that, they had often been told. Had they seen one? No, but no matter, others had. The creatures were there. Better to leave them in peace. That way they won't harm or be harmed. All deep water holds its own secrets.

The Birds and Plants of Loch Ness

IN THE EARLY years of the 20th century the birds and the flowers of the eastern end of Loch Ness were observed and lovingly recorded by a minister of the United Free Church, the Reverend Angus MacFarlane. He lived with his family in the manse at Lochend; ministered also in the church on the other side of the loch at Dores; and took services in the schoolhouse in the upland community of Abriachan. He is well remembered with interest and affection, particularly in Abriachan where he lived after his retirement. Members of his family were teachers in the school there.

He described the birds in a lecture to the Inverness Field Club, saying that he found 'many of such absorbing interest as to photograph themselves on my mind.' He adds 'the birds herein included are fairly representative of the whole area around Loch Ness, while I venture further to say that few districts of similar size can be found with such a variety of bird life.' After pointing out that the immediate shores of the loch are mostly steep and lacking in cover – rushes or sedges – for nesting, he notes the usual water birds – mallard, coot and moorhen – do find the means to survive. Black-headed gulls, which breed on the shores of the small hill-lochs, later bring their young down to Loch Ness, with much movement and clamour.

Golden plover and lapwing come in due season to the higher ground, along with the curlew. The redshank, with its 'shrill, distressful piping', the oyster-catcher and the sand-piper all liven the shore of the big loch. The heron is occasionally seen at his solitary fishing. He breeds in a heronry further to the west. The cormorant sometimes appears perched on his own on a rock or a buoy. He goes for shoals of parr as they make for the sea and gets them in the shallows at Bona, though keepers and water-bailiffs are looking out for him.

Mr MacFarlane's description of the dipper must be quoted at length:

A familiar aquatic figure... all through the winter is the dipper or water-ouzel, its white waistcoat thrown into relief by what we might style its dark brown overall. Who does not stand awhile admiring its dapper figure and lively motions – as, one moment bobbing on a boulder, shaking off the crystal drops, the next darting into the water, circling and diving, after which emerging, and perhaps finding your prolonged attentions rather irksome, it takes its flight along the shores to pastures new? ... its nesting haunt ... is generally by the side of some remote waterfall, where often the spray sprinkles the penthouse dome of the very compact, moss-built, grass-lined nest, which holds those five lovely ovals, whose satin whiteness matches that of the bird's breast...

The dipper was a favourite of John Muir, the conservationist, who writes about the bird frequently in his journals.

Mr MacFarlane tells of his sadness at finding the head and wings of a kingfisher by the roadside –

the head and wings being of that beautiful lustrous green, peculiar to the bird, barred with azure, while the cheeks and chin and underside of wings bore traces of the tints that make up the rest of the colour scheme... I could not but ask myself what had brought it this way. Was it perchance some dim memory of halcyon days, when before ruthless commerce had disturbed their peaceful solitude, converting it into a busy thoroughfare, its ancestors had bred in the shady banks of Bona? There is something quaintly attractive about this bird. Perched on its bough, the short legs invisible, the slight body dwarfed by the large head and long bill, staring down for the small finny prey that, when they rarely come, are so unerringly seized, it has a quizzical 'tout ensemble' that has always caught the limner's fancy, just as the heron's pensive attitude, from standing ankle-deep on its stilt-like legs, with its long beak poised downwards at the proper angle to strike, has also done.

The wood pigeon, with its gentle cooing, seems an inoffensive creature, though it attracts the attention of angry farmers on account of its habit of eating newly sown turnip seed. The red grouse, the partridge and the capercaillie (in Gaelic *capul coille*, 'the horse of the woods') are all found in the wooded slopes bordering the loch, along with hawks. The sparrow hawk, as its name implies, is particularly hard on small birds. Mr MacFarlane quotes a story of a sparrow hawk chasing a small bird through an open window and under a bed, defying the human occupant, who summoned the cat, which eventually, after a struggle, sent the hawk packing!

Two kinds of owl, the tawny and the barn, are less ruthless killers. The rook, the jackdaw and the raven all find nesting sites in the area, in trees or on rocks. 'Nothing short of death will prevent the raven from having eggs about Shrovetide and young about Easter' quotes Mr MacFarlane. He goes on to say: 'Superstition has put its ban on the bird with its sombre garb, its aloofness, its ominous croak. Its strong attachment to its haunt is shown in the many places called 'Raven's Rock'.'

When starlings, which had been in the habit of nesting in the loft of his house, found their way blocked by some new masonry put in to repair cracks in the wall, the birds worked their way through solid concrete to their old nest-sites, and were welcomed. The family enjoyed 'their medley of song, borrowed from mavis, blackbird and others, with their own curious throat-rattle running through.' They didn't mind the clatter and the chatter of the young birds.

Resident thrushes and blackbirds are plentiful, along with the winter fieldfares and redwings, the 'snow-birds.' Sand-martens find places to tunnel into and swallows seek out barns and the eaves of houses. Swifts are not seen. The little residents – the hedge sparrow and the robin – are fed at the door. Warblers, the stonechat, the wheatear, are welcome summer visitors. An elusive, tiny bird, the goldcrest, may be glimpsed, occasionally, in the woods. One migrant bird, in particular, caught Mr MacFarlane's attention – the redstart. He writes:

One bird we are proud to claim as an inhabitant of Loch Nessside is the redstart, than which few birds are so handsome, especially the male, which, in addition to the red tail common to both sexes, has a white patch on the forehead, a black gorget and a crimson-red breast. This colour pales on the belly and then gradually deepens, till it reasserts itself in the rich rust-red of the tail. Both male and female have the upper parts brownish-grey, the tones being lighter in the latter, which has the red of the male breast replaced by a light grey. Their nest, built in a wall (twice in the same hole, the first having been duly removed) ... has been under review for the last three seasons. It is loosely made of moss and grass, lined with wool and feathers. The eggs, five or six in number, are of a lovely apple-green tint. The hen is a model sitter, and marvellously tame, allowing one to insert a hand, and then only receding into a corner of the hole. She is relieved in her monotonous occupation by her mate singing in a tree above the nest. Though not very entrancing to human ears, I have no doubt it is sweet enough in hers. He acts the sentinel at the same time. Both are very assiduous in feeding the young, which, even after they have left the nest, are led back into it every night, for several days. After that they gradually draw them away into the deeper recesses of the wood, where they are little seen till they depart in early autumn for the Continent. I have often watched the process of feeding. Though after a while the birds lost a lot of their shyness in entering the nest, yet they never gave up the habit of reconnoitring between the trees, at the back and the parapet in front of the nest, flitting to and fro several times before venturing into the hole. The picturesqueness of the drama was enhanced at times by the male executing a sort of skirt-dance in front of the nest, immediately before entering, when it danced backwards and forwards several times in rapid succession, at the same time opening its tail in and out fan-wise with a quick, quivering motion which, when the summer sunlight shone upon it, gave it a flaming appearance, which probably accounts for two of its south-country names: Fire-tail and Fire-flirt.

Finally Mr MacFarlane describes the wren thus:

The brown wren is known to most people... No-one objects to Jenny or even Kitty Wren, but when the bird is referred to in popular bird-books as a troglodyte, it is nothing short of a libel, even though it is so unfortunate as to have that as its scientific name. It is an all-the-year-round resident and a familiar object as it flits from cover to cover about wayside banks and hedges, keeping generally near the ground. All its movements give one the impression of its weak powers of flight, yet it is known to cross wide seas ... Its tail, always cocked gives it a singular if smartish appearance ... Nothing comes amiss to it for making its nest in. Where moss is plentiful, it is generally and compactly built of it; but where the environment needs mimicry the bird is very ingenious in faking the outside in order to conceal it ... The nest is dome-shaped, being deep beneath the entrance. It lays many eggs sometimes as many as 12 or 14. Needless to say, all are not hatched. Indeed the bird, during incubation, may have destroyed three or four by pulling them out with its claws. The wren has a habit of building several nests in the course of the season, the reason being supposed to be for shelter. This makes it a rather difficult matter to find the rearing one.

Since Mr MacFarlane was writing these meticulous and charming observations of the birds of Loch Ness-side, some changes in the bird population have occurred, though not many. Different methods of cultivation in the areas surrounding the loch have meant, for instance, fewer lapwing, which like to nest near worked ground. Barn owls are fewer in number, perhaps on account of diminishing food sources. The capercaillie had become very scarce, but, with conservation now uppermost in people's minds, the numbers are increasing. Two magnificent birds which were persecuted to extinction during the 19th century are reappearing – the osprey and the red kite. The osprey nests near the loch and fishes there; the red kite flies over from its newly established breeding grounds further east. The return of these birds would have gladdened Mr MacFarlane's heart.

A few years after addressing the Inverness Field Club Mr MacFarlane gave a talk to the Gaelic Society of Inverness which he called *The Gaelic names of plants and a study of their uses and lore.*

After giving a very scholarly description of the various parts of plants, in Gaelic, he then considers them in four different aspects – those that provide food, those used in healing, those involved in magic or religious customs and those serving useful purposes in daily living.

First he considers cereals, oats being of prime importance in the sustenance of Highland people, in the form of brose, porridge, bannocks. He reminds us that Dr Johnson once said that in England oats were for horses, in Scotland for men. Then came the riposte – 'Where can you find such horses, where such men?' Barley was also grown, mainly for distilling purposes. He mentions sorrel, most often considered a weed by gardeners today, but much sought after then for soup and as a salad with its 'saltish and acid taste.' The nettle has long been a valued ingredient in broth, being full of iron. The first tender shoots were shredded and cooked with a little oatmeal. Peas were grown to make meal, and 'pease-meal' was eaten like porridge. Peas were also known to be good for the soil.

Next in importance, in older times, was the silverweed, which was dug up, the roots dried and ground into meal which could be baked. It was known as 'one of the seven breads of the Gael'. The plant, with its attractive leaf and flower, is found today all over the Western Isles. The seaweeds, in particular dulse, were valued as foods in the coastal areas. Whin, which is in flower most of the year, would be pounded and made into animal fodder in the spring when winter feed was running low. Special mills – 'whin-mills' – were used. Whin is now prolific in many parts of the Highlands.

The nodules on the roots of bitter vetch were dried and chewed, as gum is chewed today, to ward off hunger. This was important in times of food scarcity. Mr MacFarlane quotes Lightfoot, an 18th century botanist who travelled with Pennant in the Highlands and noticed this use. The nodules had, he said, a sweet taste, like liquorice and 'in times of scarcity, they have served as a substitute for bread'. The potato, since its introduction in the north in the 18th century has, of course, become vitally important as a food plant, as has the turnip, mainly for fodder, and the kale as a hardy green vegetable.

Going on to consider the plants which were used in healing, Mr MacFarlane pointed out that the Celts and the American Indians were people widely versed in the curative properties of plants. In the Highlands the great exponents of medical skills were the McBeths, a name anglicised to the Beatons. In 1408 Fergus McBeth was hereditary physician to the Lords of the Isles. Martin Martin, who travelled in the Western Isles in the 17th century and published a book about his findings, describes one Neil Beaton as a doctor who 'considers his patient's constitution before any medicine is administered to him'. He had no formal education but must have had a natural capacity for healing.

Goldenrod and comfrey, Mr MacFarlane says, were of first importance in the mending of broken bones. The leaves and flowers were made into a poultice and applied on a bandage. Feverfew, a pyrethrum – which means expeller of fever – and cuckoo-flower were eaten to cure headaches and reduce temperatures. The young leaves of the dandelion were taken as a tonic. Thyme 'imparted courage and strength through its bracing fragrance, virtues essential to kings and princes in olden times'. It made an infusion and was also used by women as a perfume, carried in bouquets and put away amongst linen.

Chamomile was good for the liver and for indigestion. Sage was valued. An old Latin saying has it: 'Why should a man die that has sage growing in his garden?'

The bog bean, with its beautiful flower, was considered a 'cure for all'. Juniper berries made an astringent drink for chest infections. Coltsfoot was also used for coughs.

In magic and religious customs St John's Wort was always considered an important plant. It was a favourite of St Columba's, as John was his favourite saint, and was used as a charm against witchcraft. The marigold was reverenced, as was the dandelion, both flowers of the sun. The meadowsweet was known to have soothing properties akin to those of aspirin today and so came to be regarded as beneficent. Lady's mantle and parsley were also so regarded.

The greatest protector of people and animals against malevolent forces was, of course, the rowan tree. Rowans were always to be found near a dwelling house, and a branch fixed to the door of the byre. The wood would never be burnt on a household fire. When Sweno the Dane was invading the country in Viking times and his men were suffering from thirst, a truce was made on condition that the Scots provided drink. They did so, putting the berries of the 'night-weed' into the water. The Danes fell into a drunken sleep and were easily slaughtered.

In Druids' times the mistletoe was looked on as sacred. The ash tree was considered to have powers left over from pre-

Christian times. Pennant says: 'In many parts of the Highlands, at the birth of a child, the nurse puts the end of a green stick of ash into the fire and, while it is burning, receives into a spoon the sap or juice which oozes out the other end and administers this to the new-born baby.'

The mullein was said to be 'Mary's healing' for asthma. The hazel was considered an unlucky tree, though two nuts found together meant good luck. The blossom was never taken indoors. There is the legend of the hazels at the fountain where the salmon came to drink. The red nuts on the hazel caused the red spots on the salmon and whoever ate of the salmon, the 'salmon of knowledge', who had partaken of the 'nuts of wisdom', was truly inspired. The aspen tree was reverenced as it was said that it provided the wood for the cross and so was ever trembling.

Ferns held charms. Fern seeds were to be gathered on Midsummer Eve. Mushrooms were always associated with the fairy folk, who were very real to many people. The foxglove, the 'folk's glove', was the fairy's thimble. The shamrock, or trefoil, represented the trinity and so was revered. The magic of flax probably emanated from the fact that it provided fibres, 'lint', for the making of linen. An old rhyme goes:

> Theft of salt and theft of seed
> Are thefts that leave no soul in peace;
> Until the fish jump on dry land
> For the stealer of lint there is no rest.

Salt, of course, was of prime importance as a preservative. Reeds were used as arrows, musical pipes and writing instruments. They were certainly worthy of respect. Moonwirt has been held in superstitious reverence among all ancient nations. Martin Martin records an instance of the people pouring ale into the sea before setting off to fish. He also records the people of Lewis wading into the sea at Hallowtide asking Shony, a Scandinavian God, 'to send us plenty of sea-ware for enriching our ground in the ensuing year'. These are two of many similar occurrences that show how pagan customs survived long into Christian times. Some have survived until today.

The first industrial use of plants mentioned by Mr MacFarlane is the production of dyes for colouring fabrics and wool. Woad – which gives a blue dye, as was used in colouring the faces of ancient tribes – and tormentil were used. Saffron gave the characteristic yellow colour of the Highlander's shirt. The yellow iris gave a red dye. Lichens were so highly valued as producers of dye that at one time they became a cash crop, being sent to the factories in Glasgow. This gave rise to the poet MacCodrum's saying: 'Cattle on the hills, gold on the stones'. Corcur gave a purple dye, crotal a reddish brown. People would put crotal in their stockings when going on a journey.

Heather was important, in fact it was more or less indispensable as it made ale, ropes, thatch, pot scrubbers, bedding. Hemp was grown and used to make ropes. Willow made creels and harness. Flax was widely grown, the fibres spun to make thread and linen. Many place-names show the locality e.g. Lag-an-lin, from Gaelic 'the hollow of the flax'.

Horse-collars were made of straw or marram grass. Panniers and chairs could also be made of straw, strengthened with strips of birch. Wicker, willow or hazel strands, woven, made cupboards and could even make structures, such as barns, as well as lining the walls of houses. 'Lobbans' were wicker frames mounted on wheels to make small carts and were in use till the early 1900s. Teasel would raise the nap on woollen cloth.

Milk dishes, churns, ladles, bowls, cups were all made of hard woods. By law, yews were to be grown in churchyards, where they would not be damaged, for the production of arrows, and, later, of boats.

Mr MacFarlane, in his observation of all the plant-life around him and in his study of the uses to which it has been put, makes it clear how utterly dependent people have always been on what the earth provides and how deep has been their regard for this bounty.

Down to the Shore and Further

A LITTLE FURTHER to the west a rough path down to the loch shore leads to a huge boulder – *Clach Mhor* – said to have been hurled across the water by a witch on the other side in order to exterminate a rival here. It fell short and landed in the loch. Magic lingers! Subsequently it was used as a lookout to watch for the coming of the steamer.

On the shore are water-worked pebbles of many colours and shapes and pieces of driftwood that can serve useful and ornamental purposes. Here too, in September and October time, there is a larder of wild food fit for any gourmet. Hazel nuts that contain more protein than eggs or cheese, field mushrooms, boletus, puffballs, chanterelles, brambles, rosehips full of vitamin C, wild garlic and mint, sloes to put in the gin or to flavour boiled potatoes, hawthorn berries. Birch bark can be eaten too.

Back to the road and a short distance on is an anchorage for boats stopping over by the Clansman, the modern hostelry built on the site of the old coaching inn or 'change-house', where fresh horses were kept to set the coach on its way. Up the hill behind this building is a well-hidden cave which harboured an 'illicit still', a still for the making of smuggled whisky. This was one of many, here and in the heights of Abriachan, which were in use during the 19th century, when money had to be found to meet the increases in rent demanded by the landlords. It was a risky business, fines or imprisonment being imposed on those caught in the act. But precautions were taken and many ploys invented to outwit the law. Juniper branches were used to make a smokeless fire and stones were hurled at the excisemen toiling up to the bothies. One Duncan Fraser in Abriachan was known as the King of the Smugglers. Once, when the excisemen were hot on his trail, he disguised his old father as a corpse, laid him out on the kitchen table, covered him with a sheet and put the telltale cask in his hand. No one would interfere with a corpse. A grandmother's skirts, plumped up as she sat warming herself at the fire, would also make a suitable hiding-place. The whisky fetched a good price in the town, if it could be got there safely, hidden in a load of peats or potatoes. Some, of course, was consumed locally. It was considered the best protection against the winter cold and also against the 'black dog' of melancholy that sometimes sits on the shoulder on dark nights.

The lochside native woodland here is now managed by the Woodland Trust. Some intrusive conifers have been felled and native trees replanted. A steep path leads up to Abriachan. It is known as the 'Funeral Road' as coffins were formerly carried shoulder-high on it from Abriachan, down to a conveyance waiting at the roadside to take them for burial at Kilmore, the parish church of the neighbouring glen. More than 40 different wild flowers and many types of lichen are found bordering this path.

The woodland further up is managed by the Abriachan Forest Trust, a group of local residents who took it over from Forest Enterprise in 1998. Here, the commercial plantings of conifers are being removed and native trees planted. Rowan, hazel, gean (wild cherry), bird-cherry, holly, even aspen at one time flourished among the birch and ash.

Paths and viewpoints over Loch Ness have been opened up. A bird-hide near the small hill loch, Loch Laide, has been built, also a dragonfly watch in the wet ground nearby. A replica Bronze Age house and a shieling hut act as rain-shelters for walkers, and a tree-house for the agile.

The next pier along the loch is known as 'Temple Pier', the temple being a one-time chapel dedicated to St Ninian. A well at the roadside was also dedicated to him. People would come to drink at this well in the hope of finding a cure for various afflictions, leaving shreds of their clothing on the bushes round about, thus discarding their ill-health, they hoped. The house by the road here was once an inn.

The village of Drumnadrochit (in Gaelic *Druim na drochaid*, 'the ridge of the bridge'), has a pleasant green which was originally a 'stance' or overnight resting-place for the drovers taking cattle to the markets in the south. A hard journey it was, on foot, with a bag of oatmeal, and perhaps some onions, for sustenance. Many of the old drove roads can be made out and followed. Some have been converted into the tarred roads we use today.

Much road making went on in the 18th and 19th centuries, as part of the government's 'civilising' process for the easier movements of troops. The drovers did not like the 'made' roads. The hard surface damaged the hooves of their cattle, which had to be shod for the journey. They damaged the drovers' feet too.

On a field near the green Highland Games are held every year in late August. They attract people, competitors and onlookers, from many parts of the world. These 'games' were once unique to the Highlands of Scotland. They are now held in many parts of the world to which Highland people have gone, particularly North America and New Zealand. They are really contests involving strength and skill. Piping, Highland dancing and general field sports are now included. There is also a marathon run of some 13 miles from Inverness and a hill race in which competitors run to a height of 1,000 feet.

'Tossing the caber' consists of flinging a huge pole to a position twelve-of-the-clock and 'putting the shot' means throwing a heavy weight over the height of a man's shoulder. It is said that these 'games' originated when men were extracting timber from the wood for building purposes, and to pass the time when waiting at the 'smiddy', the blacksmith's, for their horse to be shod.

The games field is also the shinty pitch. This Highland game is played with much enthusiasm by teams from all over the area. Highland troops stationed in America during the 18th century wars discovered that the native Americans played a somewhat similar game, which is now lacrosse, and friendly contests took place between them during lulls in the fighting.

At home it can be a wild game. Traditionally, at New Year, two teams met with up to 100 players a-side, no rules kept and no pitch, the game ending when exhaustion forced it to a halt.

On a mound near the games field is the burial place of the Grants, the family most closely associated with the area. Here, in 1825, the last great traditional funeral took place, for Colonel Grant of Moy, at which about 4,000 Highlanders gathered. Some of them must have walked over 100 miles to attend. Funerals were, and still are, occasions of great significance in the Highlands.

Opposite the games field a road towards the loch leads to the modern parish church and, further, to the burial ground and the site of the original church of Kilmore. The 17th century replacement is now ruined. In the earliest days people would remain standing during worship. Later, when pews were introduced, a verger, using a long stick, would prod those who had fallen asleep. Among the many graves in the old churchyard is one of Corporal Roderick Macgregor VC, one of the first soldiers to receive this award in 1857.

On the high ground above the village is a rock called Craig Mony. This is named for Mony, son of a king of Scandinavia, who, in the 9th century, at the time of the Viking invasions, landed on the west coast with his sister and a large force. When his vessels were cut off he retreated north to Glen Urquhart and made a stand here. Eventually he was defeated and was slain at a place in the hills now called for him Corrimony. His sister, who had hidden in a crevice of the rock during the fighting – a crevice since called 'The Bed of the King's Daughter' – survived. The people of the area took kindly to her and 'she lived among them many a day'. A descendant of hers could be the 'Norwegian Princess' buried at Kilianan. Later the Craig became a place of execution.

In Drumnadrochit, as well as shops and hotels, there are two large exhibitions, mostly concerned with the many attempts to identify the creatures in the loch. The formation of this huge expanse of water is explained visually. Faces and sayings of those who maintain they have seen something unusual there are flashed on the screen. There are visual accounts of all the efforts made to 'catch' a creature on film, with underwater photography, sonar beams and probes, flights of gliders. Yet, with all this sophisticated equipment, the end result is a large question mark, also flashed on the screen.

Over the years, many amateur photographers have managed

to get a picture of something out there. One of those most often reproduced is now thought to be a fake. So many things are involved, things which may add to the factor of wishful thinking. Turbulence occurs, heat-mist can distort, mirages are seen, deer swim, even the swimming of ducks can cause a wake. The loch goes its own way.

During the 1960s an encampment was set up near the shore, cameras and telescopes were placed at vantage points, manned by student volunteers. Eminent and wealthy professional men from America spent, and still spend, part of the year in the area. For these men the quest has become an obsession.

Just up from the village stood the house of Balmacaan, one-time residence of the Grants, now demolished, which became a shooting-lodge when part of the estate was turned into a deer-forest, and was let out to wealthy sporting tenants during the 1800s. One of these tenants, who came for many years to Balmacaan, was Bradley Martin, a wealthy American, whose lavish lifestyle gave employment to many local people, as game-keepers, ghillies, gardeners, domestic workers. His kindly disposition led him to make funds available for the building of the village hall, still in use today.

Lewiston is a village planned by a Grant laird, known as the 'good Sir James' on account of his kindly attitude to his tenants. It was named for his son, and meant for people dispossessed of their land to make way for sheep or deer. Along with a small house, each family had an allotment of ground sufficient to provide their basic food, and they could engage in paid employment on the estate or work as craftsmen, smiths, tailors, shoe-makers, masons, carpenters, weavers and so on. Sir James also established the nearby village of Milton, where the water from one source drove a sawmill, a tweed mill, a grain mill and a bobbin mill, thus providing much employment.

Further up into the hills are the falls of Divach. A lodge here, precariously perched on the edge of the abyss, was a summer place beloved by many Victorian celebrities – Lily Langtry, Ellen Terry, Anthony Trollope, Edward VII himself. Sir James Barrie stayed and is said to have got the idea for his 'Mary Rose' in this strange and lovely place.

Round the sweep of Urquhart Bay where the rivers Coilty and Enrick meet is another strange and lovely place. Here, in the area known as 'the Cover', a dense alder swamp and adjoining woodland are in the care of the Woodland Trust and have been designated a Site of Special Scientific Interest by Scottish Natural Heritage. Native alder, ash, bird cherry and willow are the dominant species of tree. In older times alder wood was valued in the making of vessels for holding liquid. The willow had many uses, especially the making of creels and baskets. The Woodland Trust is felling intrusive trees, such as the sycamore, planted by the Seafield Estate, and is also controlling the spread of Japanese knotweed, which was at one time planted in village gardens, and bishop weed, which was once used medicinally for reducing the pain of rheumatism. Woodland birds have benefited from the provision of open areas. In the bay, oyster-catchers, sandpipers, gulls, herons, dippers, goosanders and mergansers are all seen, along with the resident mute swans. Wildflowers are profuse from early spring to late summer. Butterflies and dragonflies flourish. This wild woodland is a unique and precious habitat for many forms of life.

Place-Names and People

THE CELTIC PEOPLES had an innate capacity for inventing place-names of extraordinary beauty and precision. The most prominent feature in the area of Loch Ness is the hill to the northeast known as Meallfourvonie (in Gaelic *Meall na fuar mhonaidh*, 'the hill of the cold moor'). Many names have, of course, been anglicised or rendered into alien spelling.

The Celt's intense feeling of affinity with the natural world led to his naming of every feature of his surroundings – every hill, rock, burn, and particular area of ground, be it wet, dry, stony, steep, flat. There are, in Gaelic, over a dozen different words for high ground, the type of country the people knew best. *Beinn* is a high hill, *meall* a rounded hill, *cnoc* a small hill, *àrd* a pointed hill, *druim* a ridge, *leitir* a slope, *aonach* rocky, steep ground. *Brae*, *tor* and *tom* also indicate height.

Some hills and fields were named for things that happened on or near them, thus providing links with the past. As we saw, at Drumnadrochit, the 'Bed of the King's Daughter' was the hollow where the Norwegian princess hid during the battle her brother Mony was fighting with the local people. Mony himself is commemorated at Cnoc Mhònaidh, Mony's stone, now anglicised to Corrimony, where he was killed.

An area of hill ground in Caiplich is known as Cnoc na h-

Eachdraidhe, 'the hill of history'. This is now recognised as the site of an iron-age settlement.

The basic word for a settlement being (in anglicised spelling) *bal* (from Gaelic *baile*), we find *bal mór*, a large settlement, and *bal beag*, a small one. Likewise, with *allt* meaning a burn, *ach* a field (from *achadh*), *lag* a hollow: Allt ruadh, 'the red burn', is so called because it contains iron; Achnahannet means 'the field of the holy place' (*Ach na h-Anoid*); Achintemerack is 'the field of the shamrock' (*Ach an t-Seamrag*); Lag na Cuspairean is 'the hollow of the archers'. One can see them there, laying a crafty ambush for an unsuspecting foe.

Kilmore, as the old church of Drumnadrochit is known, is not 'the church of Mary', as was supposed, but 'the big church'. *Doch*, from *davoch*, was a measurement of land and occurs in several place names, like Dochfour, an area of meadow land, and Dochgarroch, rough land. Aldourie, strangely, comes from two words meaning water, *allt* and *dobhar*, although *dobhar* can also mean dark.

Dores means 'a gloomy wood'. Boleskine is 'the place of the willow shoots', Foyers 'the place of sloping ground', Inverfarigaig is 'the confluence of the river' with Loch Ness.

Torr na Sìdhe is 'the hill of the fairies', where it was believed the little folk, those people who intrigued our ancestors, lived underground. Carn na h-Iolaire is 'the eagle's cairn', where he would perch before setting off to hunt food for the young ones in the nest. An creagan soillear is 'the shining rock', 'the rock lit up by the sun.' Grotaig, a place high in the hills beyond Bunloit, is a 'rotten place'. Does modern English 'grotty' derive from this?

Strone is from *sron*, the Gaelic for 'nose' and is the name of a sharp promontory jutting into Loch Ness near Urquhart Castle.

The name Urquhart is of Pictish origin, from *air* meaning 'in' and *cerddin* meaning 'woodland'.

Place-names often give clues to the geographical history of an area. Glen Urquhart, like so many parts of the Highlands, was heavily wooded at one time, as was the whole area of Loch Ness. Ruskich wood, west of Glen Urquhart, was known for its huge trees. Large groves of oak and birch woods bordered the loch. So much of this woodland has been despoiled over the centuries. Timber could be floated to Inverness, which, with its proximity to the North Sea, was a boat-building centre in the 13th century. A large vessel to take crusaders to the Holy Land was built there in 1297.

Much timber was, of course, used locally for fuel, for building purposes and to clear ground for cultivation. Bark was stripped for use in the tanning process, domestically and, later, commercially.

In the 18th century the York Building Company came prospecting for timber to fuel its iron smelting business. The Admiralty, also, was looking for tall, straight tree trunks to make masts for the fleet. Today, as we have seen, efforts are being made to restore much of the ancient woodland. It is possible that new place-names may emerge.

Many of those in the Loch Ness area are of Pictish origin. The Picts, one of Scotland's earliest tribal peoples, left no written records other than a list of kings. Their memorials are in the wonderful carved stones that survive in many places further east. Their history was recorded orally. The Druids maintained that writing was a bad idea as it weakened the memory; an oral tradition of story-telling and verse-speaking has persisted until today.

The Picts did of course name places. The prefix *pit-* is of Pictish origin and occurs widely, as in Pitkerrald, near Drumnadrochit, meaning 'Cyril's croft'. *Aber* or *ober* is also Pictish, for confluence, as in *aber-riachainn* – now Abriachan – the confluence of the speckled burn with Loch Ness. Pictish words and prefixes were gradually absorbed into Gaelic words.

During the 18th century when the clan lands were developing into estates – large sheep-farms, or deer forests for sportsmen – the lairds began taking clearer cognisance of the exact size and quality of their property. To help them in this they brought in surveyors. One in particular, Peter May, had beautiful maps created which can be seen today. The fields are delineated, the ground described as 'marshy' or 'pretty good pasture', rather in the style of the old oceanographers. The holdings were mostly described as 'lots'. The information gathered enabled rents to be adjusted, improvements made and so on.

After the big road-makers had done their mapping, in 1870 the Government, in the form of the Ordnance Survey, stepped in to produce official maps. It produced a 'name book' for each area, that is, a 'List of Names as written on the plan, with various modes of spelling the same names.' The difficulties for English-speaking officials encountering Gaelic place names must have been enormous. Great care was taken to ensure accuracy. Knowledgeable local people were brought in for consultation – the schoolmaster, the minister, the estate factor, the tenant himself. The various headings for the description of each place included:

'Authority for the modes of spelling; situation: Descriptive Remarks or General Observations which may be considered of interest.'

For instance, a holding, Easter Altourie, on the high ground north of Loch Ness, is noted like this:

Easter Altourie: Authority for spelling: James Mollison, factor, Samuel Ian Ferguson, schoolmaster at Dochgarroch, Mr Alexander Mackenzie, tenant. This name is applied to a farmhouse one storey high, with suitable offices attached; the whole are thatched and in good repair. E Baillie Esq, Dochfour, Proprietor.

Further editions of the maps included new information. The officials of the Ordnance Survey were considerate in their approach and were well liked by the people.

People, as well as places, were well-named in older times. This was essential as so many wore the same patronymic. Often they were known by some physical characteristic of an ancestor, such as a prominent nose, a big mouth, black hair. Often, too, the name of their place identified them. A sense of place was always vitally important. Roots were what mattered.

The Census returns, which began in 1841, may have tried to regularise things, bringing names of people and of their places into some sort of order, but names not found in any baptismal or other record were in everyday use. Thus, one William Fraser was known as Willy Balnagriasechin, from 'the shoemaker's place', where he lived; another as Bill-the-Post, named for his job.

A designation could be carried on through generations. Jimmy Taylor was a James Macdonald whose father had been a tailor, he himself a merchant seaman. The *breabadair* (weaver) was so called on account of his father's skill, though he was never near a loom. The 'boxer' played the accordion – the box. The 'swapper' dealt in barter rather than coin. The 'trapper' kept the place free of vermin and made some pennies for himself. The 'drover' was happiest taking cattle on the move.

Gentle satire was often indulged in. Anyone who thought too much of himself would be dubbed the 'laird' or the 'king'. All these names, bestowed with understanding and with wit, gave people a special sense of identity and of a close link with the community they belonged to.

The 'Good Sir James'

THE SIR JAMES GRANT who lived from 1738 to 1811 earned the epithet 'good' on account of his generous and understanding attitude to his clansmen, who had by then become his tenants, and because of his efforts to increase the fertility of his lands for the good of all who lived on them.

The Grants are considered to be of Anglo-Norman descent, having come north during the 12th century. One Sir Laurence le Grant was Sheriff of Inverness in 1263. He got lands in Stratherrick, the hill country to the south of Loch Ness. Grants remained there till 1419. Sir Laurence's son John supported Wallace and Moray. The family's help was recognised and they were granted much church land. Later, they settled in Strathspey.

In 1509 King James IV gave to John Grant of Freuchie the 'lawless place' of Glenurquhart to secure 'policia' and 'edification' among the people. John's two sons got Glenmoriston and Corrimony, as we shall see in the following chapter.

The principal centre of what had now become the clan remained in Speyside where, by 1536, a castle had been built. This later became known as Castle Grant, which stands there today. The chief and his entourage – his piper, his fiddler, his bard, his ferryman – formed the focus of clan life. He was responsible for the widows and children of clansmen killed in battle. He had powers of jurisdiction and held courts in various places. Penalties for wrongdoing could be severe: hanging for the theft of a sheep, a substantial fine for cursing or swearing in court. The Courts also regulated the prices paid for cloth or shoes and the amount of wages paid to servants. To suppress cattle-lifting people were urged to report raids. In 1623, for the protection of woods, it was forbidden to 'fire, cutt, peill, distroy, sell, dispon ony of the woudis . . . under ye pean of XL Lib' (£40 Scots.) In 1691 'cutteing of grein wood, grein suaid, killing of deare and rea [roe], blackcock and moorefoules' was forbidden.

At Castle Grant, until recently, hung a portrait by Richard Waitt of Alasdair Mór Grant, the laird's champion. As a boat is shown in the background, he is said to have been the laird's ferryman. It is told that, in his youth, he walked to London with his *curragh* (small skin boat) on his back. When he launched it on the Thames the onlookers threw gold pieces into it, which Alasdair presented to his chief, asking him to buy Lady Grant a few pins with the money.

In the Scottish National Museum is a portrait, also by Richard Waitt, of William Cumming, piper to the laird of Grant. On the banner attached to his pipes can be seen the clan motto 'Stand Fast Craigellachie'. The standard of dress and of the accoutrements of these two men shows how important they were as members of the chief's retinue.

From the 16th century, when a young Grant ran away with a daughter of the MacGregor chief, the Grants were associated with the MacGregors, offering them protection when they were later persecuted, deprived of land and forbidden to carry arms. For this the Grants themselves were penalised, anyone harbouring MacGregors incurring heavy fines.

After the Battle of Culloden, in 1746, the Grant chief of the time – Ludovic, described as 'the least worthy member of his long line' – betrayed some of his clansmen, getting them to hand in their weapons, with promises of pardon, then despatching them to the Duke of Cumberland for transportation.

It was into such a family, with its differing allegiances, that James Grant, Ludovic's son, was born in 1738. As his father lived mostly in London, he was educated at Westminster school and Cambridge University. His tutor, William Lorimer, an 'eminent scholar', kept an eye on him and reported to his father on 'the satisfactory progress of his pupil in his studies and on his exemplary conduct'. William Lorimer later became James's secretary and worked with him all his life. In 1758, at his father's wish, James was sent off to complete his education by travelling on the Continent, making the 'Grand Tour'. This was the custom of the time for young men of standing. A teacher reported to his father – 'he will, I am convinced, be an honest, a sensible and a benevolent man.' He speaks also of his 'great tenderness and sensibility'.

Returning after two years abroad, at the age of 21, James took over the running of the estate. In 1763 he married Jane Duff, a member of a family from Fife. They were to have a happy family life together for more than 40 years.

James's first achievement was to found, in 1765, on a barren moor in Speyside, a settlement known as Grantown. This was the first of several 'planned villages' which he was to set up, with a view to providing an alternative lifestyle for people subsisting on small farms. A linen manufactory was established, a town-house and a jail built, water was brought in and the roads improved. Money from the estate was contributed to this project.

Men were to work at the trades at which many of them were

already adept on a small scale – blacksmiths, carpenters, masons, shoemakers, tailors, slaters and so on. A school for girls was established, boys being already provided for. Regulations regarding cleanliness and fencing to establish boundaries were imposed. There was a fine of five shillings for each breach of a code of morality. James Grant was implementing his early ideals.

In 1773, after his father's death, he succeeded to the title. Finding the estate burdened with debt, he sold some of the outlying portions and gave up his seat as an MP for Elgin to avoid the expense of having to stay in London. He then set about the task of improving the Grant lands in Glen Urquhart and Glen Moriston, ordering William Lorimer to report on the condition of agriculture in the area.

One great advance he made was the compulsory liming of the ground. A limekiln was built at Gartally. He introduced turnips and rye grass and the potato, and encouraged the use of flax for spinning. Crops were to be grown on a rotational basis, with some ground left dormant, or fallow. Drainage and efficient tillage was insisted on. In all these ideas he was well in advance of his time.

Anxious to prevent emigration, which was then prevalent, he provided employment for men in planting trees, bridge building, road making and the construction of river embankments to cope with flooding. He abolished payment of rent in kind, discontinued services by tenants – in fact, ended the old irksome practices. He even created 34 new lots, bringing in small tenants. He encouraged people to build their houses with walls of stone rather than turf with wicker linings. He also advocated the modernisation of farm equipment. With improved roads, larger wheeled carts could replace the sleds that had been used to pull loads over rough ground. For the 'withies' – willow shoots used for reins and traces – stronger material, leather, would be used. For people accustomed to making their own devices, with whatever material was ready to hand, some of this modernisation was irksome. Sir James had his struggles!

At the end of the century, he called for a further report on the Glen Urquhart estate by the Rev James Headrick, who was an authority on mineralogy as well as agriculture. There was a craze for mineralogy at the time. Headrick did find traces of copper and lead, also ironstone and even a small outcrop of coal, but these were not exploited. He advocated the planting of yams and drilled beans, crops that were alien to the people and were not welcomed.

Headrick did not favour the small farm, objecting to the farmer being 'mason, tanner, shoemaker, carpenter, smith, weaver, tailor and peat-winner.' For men well accustomed to being 'Jacks of all Trades' some of the reforms caused a certain amount of resentment. One factor, a worthy but exacting man, Duncan Grant, was considered a 'malevolent being' and was actually set upon by some tenants on his way home from Inverness one night.

Sir James stood by his people in times of stress. In 1783, when crops were affected by bad weather or disease and rents were in arrears, he cancelled debts altogether.

In 1787 Robert Burns, who had been introduced to Sir James by Henry Mackenzie – the poet known as the 'Man of Feeling', who was the laird's brother-in-law – visited Castle Grant. In his journal, Burns speaks of travelling 'many miles through a wild country among cliffs grey with eternal snows and gloomy, savage glens... till I reached Grant Castle, where I spent half a day with Sir James Grant and family.' He found Lady Grant 'a sweet and pleasant lady.'

In 1793, when fear of invasion from France was real, Sir James mustered a company of Strathspey Fencibles, of about 500 men and officers. When threatened with having to serve in England or Ireland the men objected and staged a mutiny. Five years later they were disbanded.

In 1794 Sir James became Lord Lieutenant of Inverness and the following year, in order to secure a regular income, he took on the job of Cashier of Excise, living in Edinburgh for some time. In 1805 his wife died. Heart-broken, he survived her by six years, dying after a long and painful illness. Of his seven sons two died in infancy, one died aged nine, one died in India. He was succeeded by his son Lewis, who inherited the title Earl of Seafield from a cousin. Of his seven daughters only one, Margaret, married.

Anne Grant of Laggan wrote: 'His native strath still mourns the recent loss of a chief who retained as much of the affections of his people and as entire control of them, as was ever possessed by any patriarch or hero of antiquity.' Previously, in a volume published in 1803, she had composed a poem of 18 verses in praise of Sir James. She called him:

The tender parent, Friend sincere,
The Consort blessed beyond compare.

Colonel David Stewart of Garth, writing in 1822, in his *Sketches of the Highlanders*, says: 'He was the worthiest gentleman, the best master, the best friend, the best husband, the best father and the best Christian of the district, to which he was an honour and a blessing.' That is praise indeed from a man not given to exaggeration in his opinions.

Sir James would, I think, have been happy with the descendants of his family – men who were much in tune with the times, interested in tree-planting, in the improvement of housing, in the maintaining of traditional customs. One of his ilk, in particular, James Murray Grant, the 12th laird of Glen Moriston, was especially well liked. A Gaelic speaker, he lived simply and moved happily among his people.

Urquhart Castle

THE GREAT SQUARE tower of the castle, on its spur of rock, lapped by the waters of the loch, dominates the landscape, as it must have dominated the lives of many people over the centuries. Archaeological excavations have shown that there was a *dun*, or fort, here in prehistoric times. Later, a motte-and-bailey type of construction, that is, a hillock and courtyard, was built. The site is ideal for a fortified residence and may well have been originally the home of a Pictish nobleman. Emchat, such a man, who was converted to Christianity by St Columba in the 6th century, may have been the first governor of the fort. Its strategic position made it a place of great importance in the ever-turbulent times. The waters of the loch surround it on three sides. It commands views to the west and to the east. To the landward there is fertile ground which would have provided food and fuel.

The first recorded lord of the lands of Urquhart and so of the castle of that name, is an Anglo-Norman, Alan Durward, who in 1229 was appointed to defend the area on behalf of the king of Scots against the independent-minded men of the north. The castle served as an administrative centre, a court of justice, and a barracks, as well as a residence.

Later, under various Constables, or governors, the castle was besieged and occupied by English forces, then taken again by the loyalists and placed in the charge of Sir Alexander Forbes, a descendant of the famous warrior Conachar of Urquhart. With the English besieging the castle once again in 1304, Governor Forbes's wife, who was pregnant, dressed as a beggar and was allowed through the ranks of soldiers. She managed to reach Ireland, where her son was born. Her husband, along with the entire garrison, although in a state of starvation, rushed out to attack the invading forces but they were vanquished to a man.

By 1308 Robert the Bruce had control of the Great Glen. Then, towards the end of the 14th century, the castle reverted to the Crown and in 1384 King Robert II gave to his son Alexander his possessions in Urquhart, including the castle, for an annual duty of one silver penny. Two years later Alexander acquired Abriachan and other places. He did not pay the rent and became the lawless renegade known as the 'Wolf of Badenoch', burning the cathedral at Elgin and other churches. He eventually did penance before dying in 1394.

Much work was then done to keep the castle in repair. This was essential as more threats by independent-minded people were emerging, this time from the west, where the Macdonalds, Lords of the Isles, were seeking to extend their kingdom. During this time, when the lands of Urquhart – good, fertile lands – were passing continually between the crown and the Macdonalds, the castle buildings fell again into a state of disrepair. At last, when the Macdonald threat grew less, John Grant was given the lordship of Urquhart, with the castle, holding it from the Crown. This was in 1509 and the Grants have been in the area ever since. James IV ordered Grant:

To repair, or build, at the Castle, a Tower, with an outwork of stone and lime, for protecting the lands of the people from the inroads of thieves and malefactors; to construct within the castle a hall, chamber and kitchen, with all the requisite offices, such as pantry, bakehouse, brewhouse, oxhouse, kiln, cot, dovegrove and orchard, with the necessary wooden fences.

This gives some idea of the size of the establishment and of the busy life that went on within its walls. The tower, known as the Grant Tower, stands today, though now is partly ruinous, some of it having fallen during a severe storm in 1715.

There were troubles still to come. In 1545, the Macdonalds, now with allies among the Camerons, again besieged and took the castle and harried the people of the countryside. This became known as the Great Raid. The plunder included 2,000 cattle, 383 horses, 3,000 sheep, 2,000 goats, 122 swine, 64 geese and from the castle itself they took 'beds, feather beds, bolsters, blankets and sheets, tables, chairs, pots and pans, a chest containing 300 pounds, a brew-cauldron, fire-spits, barrels of oats and three big boats.'

At last, after the departure of the predators, some repairs were done to the castle, but soon it was no longer regarded as of strategic importance. In the more peaceful times of the 17th century landowners were living in more comfortable accommo-dation. An inventory of the contents of the castle, made in 1647, reveals the sorry state into which the place had fallen. The only items in the Grant Tower were: a bed, a small table and bench in the chambers, a large dining table, bench, table and chair in the hall, and 'in the cellar' an old chest.

A garrison held out against a Jacobite force in 1690, then, in retreat, blew up parts of the building to make it untenable. It decayed rapidly and eventually the local people got the chance to right the wrong they had for long suffered, by despoiling the place of stonework, roof-lead and timber. Many of them were prosecuted for so doing.

Finally, in 1913, the trustees of the Seafield Estate (the Grants) in accordance with instructions in the will of Caroline, Countess Dowager of Seafield, widow of the 7th Earl, handed the castle to the State for preservation.

> It is believed in the Parish that there are two secret chambers underneath the ruins of the Castle – the one filled with gold and the other with the plague. On account of the letting loose of the pestilence, no attempt has ever been made to discover the treasure.

The castle is now, of course, one of the major tourist attractions of the country. An enormous visitor centre has been built, with a car park to fit. The place has been used as a setting for films, for weddings and for other social events. Some artifacts discovered at the site, and subsequently removed to the National Museum in Edinburgh, are on loan there. In particular, an exquisite ewer, thought to have been made in Holland in the 15th century, is on display. A video gives an account of the history of the castle. In the grounds can be seen a replica of a trebuchet or siege catapult, which was used in a television film showing the operation of these giant machines in medieval times. Stones of the size used can also be seen.

To Invermoriston

ONWARD FROM THE castle, at the side of a straight stretch of road, is a cairn of local stone. This was built, at the suggestion of the people, by two local stone-masons, in memory of John Cobb, the racing driver, who lost his life on Loch Ness in September 1952 while attempting to break the water speed record in his boat *Crusader*. In a bronze plaque, designed by George Bain, a local expert in Celtic art, the inscription reads:

> On the waters of Loch Ness, John Cobb, having travelled at 206 mph, in an attempt to gain the world water speed record, lost his life in this bay, September 29th 1952. This memorial is erected as a tribute to the memory of a gallant gentleman by the people of Glen Urquhart. *Urrain do'n treun, Agus do'n iriosal –* Honour to the valiant and to the humble.

In the early morning of the fateful day there had been a slight ripple on the surface of the loch, but it disappeared and shortly before midday *Crusader* set off. The *Inverness Courier* of 30 September reported:

> She skimmed over the course, past the final mile post, but then seemed to bounce twice on the water. She recovered for a second, but next moment the horrified spectators saw the

boat plunge into the loch in a whirl of spray and foam flecked with flying wreckage. There was no audible explosion, but the boat gave the appearance of bursting apart.

His craft in smithereens, John Cobb was killed instantly. His body was recovered and brought ashore. Some wreckage from the boat was salvaged and burnt the next day on Temple Pier. Unfortunately, Cobb's speed, the first at over 200 mph, could not qualify as a record as a run in each direction would have been needed.

Some ten years after these events, in the 1960s, on the flat ground bordering the loch, opposite the fated 'measured mile', a camp was set up to accommodate student volunteers engaged in the ongoing hunt for *An Niseag*. In the long summer days and the short summer nights, when the sky hardly darkens, a 24-hour watch was kept, with powerful cameras posted at strategic points.

Scientists exploring the waters of the loch recently came on the remains of *Crusader* lying in the silt on the bottom. They were left there.

On 29 September 2002, exactly 50 years after the tragedy, a commemorative exhibition was set up in Blairbeg Hall, Drumnadrochit. Several of John Cobb's relatives were present to view the extensive range of photographic material and newspaper cuttings. A video was also shown, with commentary by people who had known John. The following day a wreath was laid at the cairn and another was cast into the water at the place where *Crusader* went down.

John Cobb will be long remembered as a man of great courage who endeared himself to the people among whom he lived by his friendliness and as a respecter of their ways. He kept the Sabbath quiet as they did, and did not seek undue publicity. He was a man after their own hearts.

Many affrays born of clan enmity, and nearly always involving disputed territory, took place in the vicinity of Loch Ness. One encounter was between those traditional enemies, the Macdonalds (or Macdonells) of Glengarry and the Mackenzies. In 1603, following a defeat over land in the west, Allan Dubh (Black Allan) led a body of Macdonalds on a Sunday morning to the church of Kilchrist, in Easter Ross, setting fire to the building and hacking the escaping Mackenzies to death. The victorious Macdonalds then set off at pace, driving captured horses and cattle before them. Soon, however, they were pursued by hastily gathered, vengeful Mackenzies who caught them unawares as they were relaxing. In the fight that followed they were slaughtered, all except Allan Dubh, who fled towards Loch Ness. Reaching a rocky gorge in the forest of Ruiskich he leapt across the chasm with a Mackenzie hot on his heels. He reached the other side. The Mackenzie tried the leap but landed precariously, grasping an overhanging sapling. Allan, turning, slashed the branch with his sword and the Mackenzie crashed to his death.

Still pursued by Mackenzies, Allan reached the shore, plunged into Loch Ness and swam away. Fraser of Foyers, on the other side of the loch, who had heard the noise of the affray, put out in a boat and rescued Allan.

He returned home and remained in hiding till the law caught up with him and his lands were declared forfeit. Eventually these lands were bought by the laird of Grant who left Allan in possession of them. These were turbulent times. Allan is buried in St Moluag's cemetery in Fort Augustus.

Below the road to Invermoriston is a cemetery that contains

many interesting old gravestones. Its circular form shows it to be of very ancient origin. One stone, inscribed *Iain a' Creagan* (John of the Rocks) commemorates a 17th century Jacobite chief who was compelled to spend years in hiding in rock caves. His house had been burnt down on account of his activities. The inscription on his stone reads: 'This stone is erected here in memory of the much honoured John Grant, laird of Glenmoriston who dyed Nov 30 1736, aged 79; and his son John Grant Younger, laird of Glenmoriston who departed this life ye 3rd December 1734, aged 35 years.' The adjoining stone records the death of the 'much honoured Janet Cameron, Lady to the honoured John Grant of Glenmoriston ... who departed this life Febry 1759, aged years.' Her age is not recorded. John Grant is described as 'a perfect chieftain'. He had 10 sons and 5 daughters, leading to 200 descendants. He was grandfather to Colonel Hugh Grant of Moy, whose funeral, mentioned previously, took place in Drumnadrochit.

There are also tales of love. Donald Macdonald (Donald Donn, 'Brown-haired Donald') of Lochaber, a 17th century reiver, a man who lived by cattle-stealing, was a frequent visitor to the area of Loch Ness. He was a handsome and brave man, often risking his life; and a poet, who never harmed the poor, or the weak. On one of his journeys, he met and fell in love with Mary, daughter of the laird of Grant, who lived in the castle of Urquhart. Communication between the two was strictly forbidden by Mary's father, but she and Donald often met in the shelter of the birch woods of Loch Ness. Hearing of Donald's latest depredation, the laird, in anger, swore 'the Devil take me out of my shoes if Donald Donn is not hanged.' Soldiers from the castle were sent to search the woods. Donald, scorning to leave the place because of his love for Mary, hid in a cave in Ruiskich wood and lived there well concealed for a considerable time. Then, receiving a message, apparently coming from Mary, he made his way to a supposed meeting at the inn at Alltsaigh. There, he was happily drinking when his enemies rushed in. Taken unawares he put up a fight, but, hopelessly outnumbered, was bound and taken to the castle dungeon. Convicted of the crime of cattle stealing he requested that, as a gentleman, he should be beheaded, not hanged like a common thief. His request was granted and so he could jest: 'The devil willt take the laird of Grant out of his shoes and Donald Donn shall not be hanged.'

Some of Donald's love poems have survived, as have some of his Mary's. His last poem reads:

> Tomorrow I shall be on a hill, without a head
> And no-one will have sympathy for me –
> Have you no compassion on my sorrowful maiden
> My Mary, the fair and tender-eyed.

Following the contour of the loch shore, the road twists and turns again before making an inland detour to the small settlement of Invermoriston – 'the mouth of the river of big waterfalls' (*mór easan*, in Gaelic). To the left, below the road, can be seen the site of a cotton mill, set up by the Commissioners for Forfeited Estates after the Battle of Culloden in 1746. It was erected to provide employment for women and so girls could be taught the skills of weaving and spinning while pursuing their education of learning to read and write. A supervisor would read aloud to the girls as they worked, a procedure much acclaimed by the educators of the time.

Spinning wheels were given out to some of the women so that they could work at home. The wheels were a comparative novelty. Before this time the distaff and spindle had been mostly used. This method was practical as the work could be done while walking and easily put aside. Some women did not take to the wheel, as working it was a sedentary job. Sadly, the setting up of the spinning-school was not a success. It closed after a few years, as the growing of flax on a large scale was discontinued.

The Invermoriston Hotel, the modern version of the old coaching inn, sits comfortably in the shelter of high ground, below the old settlement of Achnaconeran, Gaelic for 'the place of the hunting dogs'. Just by the hotel the road to the west takes off, up Glen Moriston. This is known as the Glen of Memories.

The Glen of Memories

AFTER THE DEFEAT of the Jacobite army at Culloden, Prince
Charles took to the heather. It was not long before he found
himself in hiding in a cave at Corrie Dho, being cared for by the
'seven men' of Glenmoriston: Alexander Macdonald, Alexander
Chisholm, Donald Chisholm, Hugh Chisholm, Grigor
MacGregor, John Macdonald and Patrick Grant. These were
among the many who consistently refused to accept the bribe of
£30,000, a vast amount in those days, for handing the Prince
over to the authorities.

As enemies of the regime they were compelled to live as out-
laws. Taking the Prince in charge, they swore to stand by him
till death. He called them his Privy Council. It was a rough life
in the cave, sleeping on a bed of heather, faring on oatmeal and the
produce of the chase. A description of the Prince, made at the
time, says 'he was barefooted, had an old black kilt-coat on, a
plaid, philibeg and waistcoat, a dirty shirt and a long red beard, a
gun in his hand, a pistol and a dirk by his side.' He had to sleep
in his clothes, though he needed little rest. He suffered from
dysentery, yet was pleasant, kindly, gallant. He remained cheerful
and hopeful, doing the cooking himself, saying his prayers in the
morning, sometimes rebuking his companions for swearing!
Eventually he continued on his way to the west. The 'seven

men' were dispersed, some overseas to Canada. Some returned, eventually, to Glen Moriston. Patrick Grant went to Edinburgh and was able to give an account of events after the battle of Culloden to Bishop Forbes, who recorded it in his book *The Lyon in Mourning*. He also returned to the glen.

A tragic incident occurred up the glen, when a party of soldiers on the constant lookout for the Prince came on a young man in Highland garb, a young man who bore a striking resemblance to their quarry. They immediately took aim. Surrendering, he shouted 'You have killed your Prince!' and fell dead. He was, in fact, Roderick Mackenzie, a Jacobite soldier from Edinburgh and one of the Prince's bodyguards. He was decapitated and his head taken to Cumberland, who dispatched it to London where it was received with great acclaim. This subsided when the truth was revealed. Mackenzie's headless body was buried at the roadside, where the small grave can still be seen. It is now appropriately marked and a cairn has been erected at the spot where Mackenzie fell.

The glen produced many men of action but it also produced poets and pipers. Poetry and music being essential elements in the old Highland way of life, the chief held his bard and his piper in high esteem. They were recorders of clan history in their telling of events in words and music.

When chieftainship died away the poets told of happenings in the community and the tunes were composed accordingly. The man known as the Glen Moriston bard was Archibald Grant, who had inherited the gift from his father, one of a noble line. He was born at Aonach in 1785 and became a tailor. Archie Taillear, as he was known, would ply his trade in the homes of the various families for whom he was making clothes and so became well known in the area. He told about people and events and was skilled as a nature poet, a love poet and a satirist. Some of his poems were recorded and published in a small volume. When he died in 1870 the *Inverness Courier* wrote of him:

> The Bard, though totally uneducated, was full of traditional story, could compose very spirited verses of poetry and his wit and humour and fun were the delight of his countrymen at all meetings such as weddings, funerals, christening banquets, rent gatherings ... he was so well liked in the glen that he was allowed to graze so many sheep gratis on every farm.

A famous piper from the glen was Finlay Macleod, piper to the 12th laird of Grant, James Murray Grant, a much-loved laird who had fluent Gaelic and mingled freely with the people. Finlay was the son of a 'herd' and was in touch with the 'tinkers'. These were men descended from 'smiths' – tinsmiths, silversmiths, goldsmiths – and many were skilled at their trade and were good pipers who knew the real old music of the pipes. Finlay joined the army and took part in the Peninsular War, when he once played non-stop while walking for 27 miles.

William Lorimer, who was tutor and later secretary to Sir James Grant, says

> there has always been a piper in Urquhart, belonging to the family of Grant, whose salary has been constantly paid by a small portion of oats from each tenant. The tenants want to get free of this tax but ... as the tax is small and being in use to be paid, it is not very sensibly felt. If you let it drop the highland Musick is lost, which would be a great loss in case of a civil or

foreign war and such Musick is part of the appendages of the Dignity of the Family. The commons are much pleased with this Musick and the use of it will be a means of popularity amongst some.

To the Fort and the Abbey

RETURNING TO THE village of Invermoriston the road curves towards Loch Ness, passing a place known to few, as it is unmarked – Columba's Well. Though sadly overgrown and no longer accessible, as the descent is considered unsafe, it can be seen from the roadside and still flows clear. When Columba was in the area he found that the people considered the well unclean, possessed by evil forces, whereupon he washed his hands in the water, took a drink and blessed the spring. Thereafter no harm came to anyone who drank of it. This was common practice in the early days of Christianity – to replace evil with good, superstition with sanctity – and it often made converts.

Passing the old smiddy, where a family of Macdonalds worked for many years, the old wheelwright's rim-maker can still be seen, though the building is now a craft shop. The road reaches the river. Upstream are the rushing waters of one of the many falls and here is the old bridge built by Thomas Telford in 1813. It is in a ruinous state but the beautiful lines of the structure still strike the eye. A walk downstream through the woodland leads to a gazebo, one of those little Victorian follies, built precariously on the rocks as a viewpoint for the waterfall.

Back to the big loch and glimpses of the water lying there, mirror-calm and blue, or flecked with white horses riding the grey crests, depending on the whim of the wind. In winter, when the trees are bare, the water seems perilously near, as though ready to rise and engulf the land. So far, its only risings have been of a few feet, and calculable, after man's intervention or floods. Other lochs, hill lochs, their waters manipulated by man with dams and sluices in order to feed our insatiable appetite for power, have swamped acres of shore and drowned the houses of the people. Here, even in summer, the canopy of leaves only half-hides the water. The sound of it, the scent of freshly washed, moss-covered rock, evidence of its presence, is always there.

The road still twists, dipping and rising, between steep rock and tree-clad slopes, as it nears the end of the loch. Before this point, Cherry Island, lying about 150 feet offshore, is glimpsed through the trees. It is the only island in the loch and is not, in reality, a natural island but a crannog, an artificial island created by man. Crannogs were built during the Bronze Age and many were in continuous use for centuries as fortified retreats and secure dwelling-places. This one would have been much larger than its present remains, before the raising of the water level by the work on the canal. It is thought that the English name 'Cherry' was given to the island by some of Cromwell's troops who were stationed in the area, perhaps on account of a gean, or wild cherry-tree, growing there. Its original name is *Eilean Mhuireach*, 'Murdoch's Island.' The Frasers used the structure as a fort. It is said that in the 16th century a Glengarry chief was invited over, then treacherously murdered by Thomas Fraser in a discussion that became a dispute over the eternal question of land. Another version of the story is that a Glengarry chief was in love with Fraser of Lovat's daughter. Her father would not hear of the match. Glengarry swam out to the island. Fraser stabbed him in the back. His followers were also killed. Their graves could, for many years, be seen on the loch shore.

In 1908 Dom Odo Blundell, a monk at the nearby Abbey at Fort Augustus, a keen historian and archaeologist, borrowed a heavy diving suit and lead-lined boots from the Canal people and investigated the construction of the 'island'. He found a pile of oak logs on the bed of the loch, covered by a layer of heavy stones and retaining posts, clearly the foundation of a substantial building. He also found traces of a causeway, now submerged. This is the first instance of underwater archaeological investigation.

A few years ago a pathway to the loch shore was made, leading to a viewpoint where Cherry Island can clearly be seen. An attractive plaque here shows how the original crannog became a fort, and depicts the story of what happened there over the centuries.

From this point a good view is also obtained of Horseshoe Crag on the opposite shore of the loch. This is a rocky slope, relatively inaccessible to man and grazing animals, and is a rare example of what primeval forest must have looked like. Birch is dominant and on the more fertile ground oak, ash, hazel and aspen grow. Scots pine, holly and juniper do well on thinner, acid soils and among the trees there is a profusion of plants of many kinds – bugle, wood sage, blaeberry, golden rod, wild strawberry. This is a hidden paradise for wild life of many kinds.

A mile or so further on from Cherry Island rises the tower of the Abbey of Fort Augustus. The original name of the settlement surrounding the Abbey was *Kilchumein*, 'the chapel of Cumein', the early Christian missionary who came here in the 6th century. Many people living in the village would like to see the ancient name reinstated. This was a place where, in the 18th and 19th centuries, drovers would congregate before taking their cattle over the Corrieyairick pass to the markets in the south. It had always been a place for meetings, for the exchange of goods and of news and gossip. It was to become a garrison, a place for the containment of soldiery and all that that entails.

A wall of the original fort, built after the uprising of 1715, can be seen in the grounds of the Lovat Arms Hotel. In 1729 General Wade abandoned this structure and rebuilt the fort nearer to Loch Ness, on the site of a much older building that had belonged to the Frasers. He then changed the name of the settlement to Fort Augustus, this being the name of a son of George II. This Augustus later became the notorious Duke of Cumberland. The line of places known by names beginning with 'Fort' were all called after the King's progeny, thus Fort William, Fort Augustus and Fort George, the latter originally in Inverness, then moved further east on the Moray Firth. These forts were designed as garrisons for troops to deal with the Highlanders of the 'Wild West' after the Jacobite rebellions of 1715 and 1745; it was after these risings that General Wade was commissioned to build roads and bridges in many parts of the Highlands. Some of the lairds disapproved of this as they reckoned the roads would make an unwelcome intrusion into the privacy of their estates and the bridges would turn people accustomed to wading the fords into weaklings.

General George Wade, who was to be appointed Commander-in-Chief in Scotland, came to the Highlands in 1724 to establish order among the people. After due consideration of the situation he concluded that the building of roads and bridges would be a valued means of 'civilising the Highlanders', as he put it in his first report to the king.

The roads were, of course, built primarily to facilitate the movement of troops. These troops were largely townsmen, recruited from among the less reputable ranks of society and totally unused to the conditions in the Highlands and to the ways of the people living there, whom they were taught to consider barbarians, perhaps in order to make killing them easier.

Fort Augustus could accommodate 300 men, with a house for the Governor and one for the Galley-Master, an important man whose job was to see to the sailing of the boats bringing supplies from Inverness. One Galley-Master, Mark Gwynne, sailed the galley for 27 years and was eventually drowned in the loch during a storm. His grave can be seen in the village churchyard.

In March 1746 rebel forces fired a lucky shot from what became known as 'Battery Rock' just east of the fort, which caused the explosion of the powder magazine. The men of the garrison surrendered and were taken prisoner.

A month later, after the Battle of Culloden, on Culloden moor east of Inverness, when the Jacobite troops were routed in the unequal struggle with the Duke of Cumberland's forces, the fort was reoccupied. Subsequently, the Duke made it his headquarters.

Simon Fraser, Lord Lovat, was imprisoned in the fort before being sent to London for trial and execution. He was proud to the end and prayed that the women of the Highlands would 'cry the coronach' over his remains. He left money for every piper in the country to play a lament.

Nine regiments were then stationed at the fort to do 'the work of vengeance'. This meant the harrying and despoiling of the glens, the massacring of men, women and children in an attempt finally to exterminate or subdue the 'riotous clans'. One instance of individual rearguard action has been recorded. Alexander Macdonald, known as Gorrie, a notorious cattle-lifter whose refuge was in a cave near Glendoe, on the south shore of the loch, not far from the fort, was determined to do what had been left undone at Culloden – assassinate Cumberland. The Duke had survived a near miss at the start of the battle. Now Gorrie saw his chance. Cramming his blunderbuss with lead, rusty nails, scrap iron, he lay in wait for the Duke to pass on the way to the fort, adjusting his weapon in the fork of a tree. Soon he heard the clatter of hoof-beats and the jangling of harness of the approaching cavalcade – the Duke and his bodyguard, red-coated, their gilded accoutrements flashing in the sun. He took aim, but, his nerve shaken, he missed. He fled to his cave, followed by a small detachment of soldiers. For many days they stood guard at the entrance to his abode, but it was well provisioned and Gorrie was able to outstay their surveillance. He remained there in the inner fastnesses, until, falling ill, he was taken by his wife to end his days in the village.

Meanwhile, the work of subduing the natives was going on. One regiment, Kingston's Horse from Nottinghamshire, 'went a-rummaging up and down the glen, destroying all the ploughs, harrows, etc., pots, pans, household furniture, not excepting the stone querns with which the people grind their corn.'

There was one betrayal of the people by their own chief. On 4 May 1746, Ludovic Grant received the surrender of 16 men of Glen Urquhart and 68 of Glen Moriston, on the promise of protection. They were handed over to Cumberland, sent to Inverness, then to Tilbury, London, and subsequently shipped off to the Barbados. Only seven or eight were ever able to return home. The names of all these men have been recorded.

To feed the large number of troops in the fort and in the

surrounding camp, up to 2,000 head of cattle were brought in. To keep them in good spirits, wild sports, horseracing with local women riding bareback, wrestling and so on, were engaged in. General Wolfe expressed horror at the orgies he saw.

The use of arms, the playing of the pipes and the wearing of the traditional Highland dress were forbidden. Men were bound by a shameful oath:

> I do swear as I shall answer to God at the great day of judgment, that I have not, nor shall have, in my possession, any gun, sword, pistol or arm whatsoever and that I never use tartan, plaid or any part of the Highland garb; and if I do, may I be cursed in my undertakings, family and property; may I never see my wife and children, father, mother or relations; may I be killed in battle as a coward, and lie without Christian burial in a strange land far from the graves of my forefathers and kindred; may all this come upon me if I break this oath.

Teaching in the schools was to be in English. The school set up in Fort Augustus had to be closed after a few years, as the children, whose only language was Gaelic, could make no progress in their learning.

In order to facilitate the movement of troops, Cumberland set about the making of maps. One of the men engaged in this task was William Roy, whose maps became well known and formed the basis for the Ordnance Survey maps of today.

Gradually, as the Government's fear of insurrection decreased, the number of men in the fort, the 'garrison' as it was known, also grew less. Many developments were taking place in the area. There was some emigration, some men joined the army, thus allowing them to wear the tartan and carry a gun, and people were being encouraged to settle in villages and work at crafts. In the last years of the 18th century, Thomas Telford, the great engineer, arrived on the scene with a remit to open up the Highlands.

One colourful 19th century Fort Augustus character was Roualyn Gordon Cumming, a famous lion-hunter, who wrestled a bull at Borlum. He had a museum of African trophies and would greet tourists grotesquely dressed.

In 1834 the cannon were removed from the fort and it was left in charge of a few veterans. Finally, in 1867, it was sold to Lord Lovat who used it for a time as a shooting lodge before handing it over to Benedictine monks. The former parade ground was turned into a green space, surrounded by cloisters. The monks, some of whom came from various parts of Europe, made a garden, kept bees, held services in a beautiful chapel. Many were men of exceptional intellectual ability. In 1890 they constructed the first hydroelectric scheme in the country. Spare capacity was used to provide street lights in the village until 1951. One monk in particular, became a skilled weather forecaster, a useful asset in an agricultural community.

In 1919 the monks decided, in order to maintain their way of life and also the fabric of the building in which they lived, to open a school. About 100 boys, many from overseas, were to be educated there and to enjoy the freedom of the large playing fields, boating on the loch and expeditions into the surrounding hills and glens. Sadly, in 1993, the costs of maintaining the huge building, of providing heating and so on, forced the closure of the school. For some years it was used as a visitor centre, with audio-visual displays and other modern technological devices, a restaurant and a shop, but still the costs outweighed the revenue

The village of Foyers, seen from Easter Boleskine.
(Photograph courtesy of Rosemary Holt – www.tinkerbell-images.co.uk)

Inverfarigaig beach.

(Photograph courtesy of Rosemary Holt – www.tinkerbell-images.co.uk)

Dun Dearduil at Inverfarigaig.
(Photograph courtesy of Rosemary Holt – www.tinkerbell-images.co.uk)

The *Gondolier* and her crew.

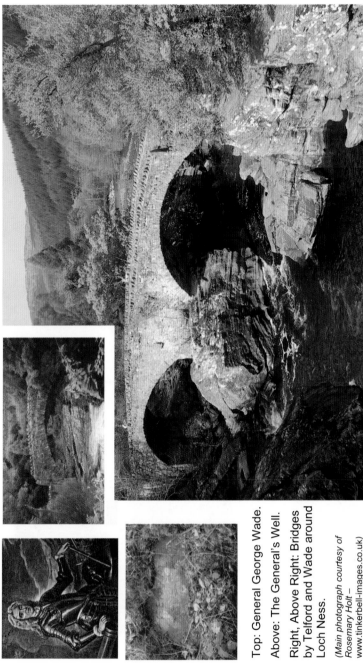

Top: General George Wade.

Above: The General's Well.

Right, Above Right: Bridges by Telford and Wade around Loch Ness.

(Main photograph courtesy of Rosemary Holt – www.tinkerbell-images.co.uk)

Sunset at Dores.

(Photograph courtesy of Rosemary Holt – www.tinkerbell-images.co.uk)

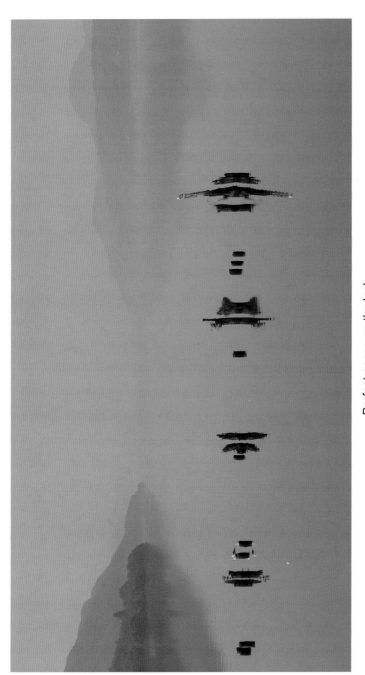

Perfect peace on the loch.
(Photograph courtesy of Rosemary Holt – www.tinkerbell-images.co.uk)

Urquhart Castle.
(Photographs courtesy of Rosemary Holt – www.tinkerbell-images.co.uk)

and the much-loved place had to revert to the Lovat estate. The remaining monks found refuge elsewhere. The library of 40,000 books, many quite irreplaceable, had to be dispersed, some, thankfully, to the National Library in Edinburgh, some to the College of Theology in Dingwall.

The Abbey buildings have now, after much restoration, been made into residential accommodation. The local people are glad that there will be life about the place again.

The Canal

IN 1801, THOMAS TELFORD, a brilliant engineer, was asked by the Government to prepare a survey on the state of communications in the Highlands. A countryman by birth, the son of a Lowland shepherd, he had started life as a stonemason and became a surveyor, an architect, an engineer. He entered on his new task with much enthusiasm.

The building of roads and bridges in the still almost trackless country was to be a key factor in promoting law and order and, it was hoped, in promoting industrialisation and preventing emigration. The Highland people, as we have seen, did not take easily to the new roads, finding the gravel surfaces hard on the feet of their horses and cattle, and on their own feet too, forcing them to wear shoes. But the building went on and the greatest single enterprise to be undertaken was the construction of the Caledonian Canal, the linking of the three lochs – Loch Lochy, Loch Oich and Loch Ness – to form a navigable route from east to west.

This would cut out the dangers of the perilous voyage through the Pentland Firth, where storms and French privateers were always lurking, and was to be of strategic value in the war against Napoleon, which was still raging.

Edmund Burt, an engineer who was working in the Highlands in the 18th century, had discussed in 1725 the feasibility of the formation of a canal, but had doubts about storms, floods and so on. In 1774, Pennant, a traveler, had similar doubts. James Watt, of steam-engine fame, surveyed the line of lochs on behalf of the Commissioners for the Forfeited Estates, but considered the idea too ambitious and costly.

The Brahan Seer, a well-known Highland prophet, had predicted in the 17th century, 'strange as it may seem to you this day, the time will come, and it is not far-off, when full-rigged ships will be seen sailing eastward and westward by the back of Tomnahurich at Inverness.'

So, in 1803, work began on this tremendous undertaking. Fort Augustus became a place of great activity, situated as it was in a central position along the route. The prospect of paid employment brought in labourers from a wide area, as well as some skilled tradesmen, masons, carpenters. The labouring work was hard, pick, shovel and barrow being the tools employed. For men unaccustomed to working set hours, particularly in winter, it was irksome. The craftsmen were reasonably well housed but for the rest living conditions were primitive, sleeping in turf huts, with the barest of rations, largely oatmeal, and a small dram of whisky for those 'working in the water'. As most of the men came from crofts, which had to be attended to, they were obliged to absent themselves at times of harvest, sowing, peat-cutting, and so on.

In his first Report, in 1804, Telford says, 'the people have already, with considerable facility, fallen into the necessary modes of employment and will soon, I have no doubt, acquire habits of industry which will prove a lasting benefit to themselves and may be expected to improve that part of the United Kingdom and put a final stop to the spirit of emigration.'

A poem, written lately by Ian Blake, gives a picture of the navvies:

Ascending Neptune's Staircase

Eight slabs of water step us from the sea,
'the narrows' and the cleanly-cut canal
confined between high, water-acned walls
of hewn red blocks so skilfully aligned.
Water – held at bay by oak-beamed gates,
sluices raised – boils black beneath our keel,
furious in its impotence.

We scarcely feel
our slow ascent towards that rectangle
of solid blue which roofs our watery cell
until we match the level of the loch –
float free above the sea we left behind –
where once blunt, butty coasters pushed and nudged
salt-bleached ocean-goers, barges big with coal,
lumpish, threading green pine-pleated skirts
of mountain scree which sweeps down to embrace
bottomless waters, astonishing the gaze
of reticent wild-cat, marten, antlered deer.

Rafted together, fourteen pleasure craft
imperceptibly inch-up past ashlared blocks,
sole legacy of long-dead navvies whose
crowbars shouldered fresh-cut stone in place,
long-handled shovels sliced through cake-damp peat,
pickaxes sparked glaciated rocks.

Their bone and muscle dug for twenty years,
the *Navigable road,* built Telford's locks,
for half-pennies-an-hour; across a sea,
to wives and children planting blighted fields,
it seemed a fortune, such their poverty.
Beside the channel they reamed-out, these men –
'the navigators' – ate, slept, year by year,
in sodden benders formed from hazel boughs,
pervious hessian which thin, mean, mizzling rain
invaded as it drenched their sweat-rank clothes.

Skin tanned dark by wind, sun, peaty fires,
day-after-day, midge-maddened, never wholly dry,
spit by spit they labour on or die –
malnourishment, exhaustion, struck by years,
consumption, accident, or desperate hand –
names unchiselled.
No smooth-polished plaque,
mute monument, alerts the visiting eye
to their long-lost interments, work-worn lives;
only this rippling highway, sea to sea,
beside which those first, ragged, navigators lie.

It had been at first thought that land required for the formation of the canal would be easily obtained, when the advantages
it would bring were realised. But several landowners made objections to the work. Macdonell (Glengarry) claimed disturbance
of fishing and loss of amenity on Loch Oich, and even sent men
out at night to destroy work done during the day. Further east,
Evan Baillie of Dochfour claimed £445 on the grounds of loss of

salmon and trout for his household. Lady Saltoun of Ness Castle claimed £5,547 for damage to net fishing, loss of value of meal and barley and for shortage of water for the sawmills. Eventually, in 1825, Parliament insisted that detailed claims for compensation must be formally lodged within the year.

Similar claims were to be made later in the century at the coming of the railways, and in the 1950s at the arrival of hydroelectric activities.

In spite of difficulties the work proceeded. Some Irish workers were brought in. A brewery was set up at Corpach 'that the workmen might be induced to relinquish the pernicious habit of whisky-drinking and cows are kept at the same place to supply them with milk.' To reduce costs in some parts oxen were used instead of horses to draw wagons.

Timber and stone were produced locally, the logs being floated down the rivers and lochs, sometimes jamming and causing damage. There was dredging and leak patching and planting of trees such as whin and broom to hold the banks together. These still bloom today.

Near Fort William, at Banavie, much work was involved in the adjusting of the water level. Here, a flight of eight locks raises the Canal by 62 feet. This is known as 'Neptune's Staircase' and was described by the Poet Laureate, Robert Southey, as 'the greatest work of art in Britain.' Southey was travelling in the Highlands at the time and became a friend and admirer of Telford. A poem he wrote in praise of the great engineer may be seen engraved in marble on a wall at Clachnaharry, the eastern end of the canal. Telford, who was a man of many talents and interests and was unfailingly good-humoured in spite of many setbacks and problems, would have enjoyed the company of Southey.

With the Napoleonic wars ending in 1815, doubts about the completion of the canal began to arise. In 1818 the bridge at Drumnadrochit was damaged by 4,000 birch logs swept along by floods. But, in spite of problems and rising costs, the work continued and in 1820 a passage from the sea in the Beauly Firth to Loch Ness had been opened and a steamboat was plying regularly between Inverness and Fort Augustus. The village, with its 200 or so canal builders – masons, carpenters, blacksmiths, quarrymen, labourers – became a very busy place indeed and, with its stagecoach connection to Fort William, was firmly on the traveller's route.

At last, in 1822, the whole Canal was opened. The first passage from sea to sea in a steamboat was on 23 to 24 October and took 13 hours. Mr Charles Grant the MP and the Commissioners and Magistrates of Inverness were on board, with a number of country gentlemen. The *Inverness Journal* reported:

> The vessel started from Muirtown locks, amidst the firing of guns and the music of the Inverness Militia band, and seemed to have kept up a running fire of guns all the way, which was returned on passing by Dochfour. The reverberation of firing repeated and prolonged by a thousand surrounding hills and rocks, the martial music, the shouts of the Highlanders and answering cheering of the party on board produced an effect which will not soon be forgotten by those present.

The party dined in the Schoolhouse at Fort Augustus and had another grand dinner, with gunfire and a bonfire at Fort William.

Telford, at the onset of the great project, had estimated the cost at £350,000 and the time required at seven years. The time-span had risen to nearly 20 years and the cost had multiplied to over a million pounds. The number of men employed had risen from 150 to 900. There were problems still to be overcome. In 1838 a dock wall at Fort Augustus fell in. There was dilapidation thought by some to have been caused by the hurried finish and hasty opening of the canal. In 1846 the people of Inverness were alarmed by the possibility of flooding and the canal was closed for a time.

Repairs were made and life went on busily on the water. Fishing boats came through from the west, produce of all kinds was carried and passengers travelled happily, entertained by performers on the canal side such as 'Paddy', the Irishman who danced and sang in return for a few coins. At Inverness carriages would await the arrival of the steamer, providing transport to the town centre.

In 1866 the paddle steamer the *Gondolier* was launched. She and her sister-boat the *Glengarry* were to carry passengers on Loch Ness for many years. Local men found employment as seamen, stewards, dockers. The *Gondolier*'s most famous passenger was Queen Victoria, who, on 16 September 1873, sailed aboard her from Fort Augustus to Dochgarroch. Of her trip, she said: 'The Caledonian Canal is a very wonderful piece of engineering but travelling on it is very tedious.' This is a reference to the waiting time at passage through the locks. Evidently, on her day of travel, there were no entertainers to relieve the tedium.

Such a huge construction needs, of course, to be kept in good condition. Repair work on the locks goes on continuously. It is hoped that funds will always be available for maintenance and improvement. In Fort Augustus a small exhibition run by the Waterways Board gives information about the building of the canal, alongside some artefacts and a model of the *Gondolier*.

Today, boats of all kinds appear on Loch Ness, from canoes to yachts and pleasure cruisers. Sadly, at small places like Abriachan, Inverfarigaig, Foyers, where mail and goods of all kinds were landed and taken aboard, along with passengers, the piers have disintegrated since the early 1930s. But there is plenty of leisure activity – racing, water-skiing, the ongoing search for the elusive *Niseag*. Some hardy swimmers try, and occasionally succeed, in swimming the length or the breadth of the loch. One gigantic vessel, the *Lord of the Glens*, takes people on a seven-day cruise to Oban and the west. In 1991, 37 Tall Ships passed through the canal as did, three years ago, the replica *Golden Hind*. These were days to remember.

The Forgotten Railway

IN THE MID 1800s, when 'railway mania' was rampant in many parts of the country, several schemes for running a line through the Great Glen were mooted. By 1855 trains were running between Inverness and Nairn. Ten years later the Highland Railway Company was established, with headquarters in Inverness. Hotels were opened, such as the well-known hostelry in Inverness where many notable people have stayed on their visits to the Highlands, mostly in pursuit of deer or salmon. Railway enthusiasts insisted on the benefits to the community of this new mode of transport, though the difficulties of making cuttings through mountainous country were clear.

Railway companies were springing up everywhere and there were no fewer than eight schemes to run a line through the Great Glen. Finally, in 1896, the Invergarry and Fort Augustus Railway Company fought off competition from rival companies, survived a protracted Parliamentary battle, and was free to operate a line of 24 miles connecting the existing track at Spean Bridge to Fort Augustus. Lord Burton was the principal instigator and put up half the capital. A light railway would have sufficed, but the line was engineered to main line standard, with a double track, two viaducts, bridges and some tunnelling, with elaborate stations and big yards. This was all set up in a sparsely populated, mountainous area. And an extension was built, with the line going on to a further station and a pier at Loch Ness, where, it was planned, passengers could embark on a steamship bound for Inverness.

In 1901 the line was ready to become operational, but by then, after the lavish spending on the construction, no funds were left for the purchase of engines and rolling stock. The rival companies began to clamour again for supremacy. There were more Parliamentary debates. In 1903 the Highland Railway Company took over the working of the line, the Invergarry and Fort Augustus people investing, typically, in a gold whistle which was blown to set off the first train! Troubles soon beset the new operators. Lack of trade and loss of shareholders forced a withdrawal of the Company and a take-over by the rival North British Railway Company in 1907. The people of the area were remarkably loyal to their railway. Public meetings were held up and down the Great Glen to try to find ways and means to save it. Some of the large landowners, however, were not so anxious to promote any railway. The idea of a noisome file of carriages, pulled by an engine billowing smoke, passing within sight and earshot of their homes, was anathema. The deer, they said, would be terrified. Others thought the 'noisome carriages' might bring more clients to hire their shootings and fishings. The discussions make interesting reading, as they are recorded in the annals of Westminster debates.

This troubled little line was closed again in 1911, then reopened two years later. Efforts to sell the material for scrap had failed. Trains carried passengers until 1933, then freight only until 1946, when the line finally closed.

The amount of motor traffic had increased greatly over the years and lessened the demand for a through rail link. Traces of the line can be seen in an embankment at Lord Burton's house at Dochfour and beside the road from Fort Augustus to the west. The elaborate pillars of the viaduct at Fort Augustus are still there, though the station has gone. The line along Loch Oich makes an attractive walkway.

It is interesting to note that Telford was not in favour of 'rail roads'; of vehicles moving in trains on fixed tracks. He preferred the idea of 'motor carriages'. Perhaps he foresaw the advent of the automobile.

Thomas Telford

THOMAS TELFORD WAS born in 1757 in a cottage in Eskdale, in
the Scottish Borders, the son of John Telford, a shepherd, and
his wife Janet. Three months after his birth, his father was dead.
He and his mother moved to live in a single room in a dwelling
shared by a neighbour. His uncle paid the small fees which allowed
Thomas to attend the local parish school and there he made good
friends, to one of whom, Andrew Little, he remained faithful all
his life. Spare time and long summer holidays from school he spent
working for farmers, sometimes staying for weeks in shepherds'
bothies in the hills. This gave him an intense love for his native
place, a love that never left him.

On leaving school Thomas was apprenticed to a mason and
his first work with the chisel was to inscribe a memorial on his
father's gravestone. He had grown tall and sturdy, with thick, dark,
curly hair, and was known to his friends as 'Laughing Tam' on
account of his good and happy nature. He was befriended by a
Miss Pasley who, having heard of his literary aptitude at school,
gave him the run of her library. There, he found *Paradise Lost*
and the works of Burns, which he read avidly and which gave
him a life-long love of reading and writing poetry.

At the age of 23 he walked to Edinburgh to seek work. Two
years later he was off to London on a borrowed horse, with all

his worldly possessions in a saddlebag. There, with letters of introduction, he made the acquaintance of many architects, including Robert Adam, and soon got work on the building of Somerset House. He spent hours studying to become an architect and in 1787 was appointed Surveyor of Public Works for the County of Salop. By then he was able to send money to his mother and to Andrew Little. He lived very simply, 'drinking only water, avoiding all sweets and having sowens and milk for supper.' He continued reading avidly, determined that literature, art, the work of the imagination should combine with the work of the scientist, the engineer, in the planning of the built environment.

Telford's next appointment, in 1793, was that of General Agent, Engineer and Architect to the Ellesmere Canal Co., an appointment which was to change the course of his life. The Industrial Revolution had meant the setting-up of factories and the transporting of raw materials and finished goods to and from these factories. The roads in the country being in a dire state of disrepair, canals, which could carry heavily laden boats and barges, were to be developed. 'Canal mania' set in.

Telford's contribution to this great endeavour was ten years' labour in the building of the Shropshire aqueduct of Pont Cysyllte, the 'stream in the sky', a huge iron trough on pillars of stone, rising high above the valley, the marvel of the time. The structure still stands today. By then he was kept incessantly busy, acting as consultant on many engineering works, yet he still found time for study, for reading for pleasure and for writing verse. The death of Robert Burns in 1796 affected him greatly.

In 1784 the Highland Society had been formed, as concerns grew about conditions in the Highlands following the breakdown of the traditional way of life. The British Fisheries Society was set up, with a view to developing a Highland fishing industry by building small fishing ports. At last, in 1801, the Government took action, appointing Telford as engineer to the Fisheries Society, to survey and report on the state of affairs in the Highlands. Part of his remit was to investigate the causes of emigration from the area. As a countryman he could see at once that the creation of sheep walks was restricting the traditional way of rearing cattle. An alternative means of living for the people had to be found. This could be by developing the fishing and providing roads to convey the seafood to the inland markets. Roads, of course, involved bridges, the harbours had to be upgraded and the proposed canal through the Great Glen would unite the fishing grounds of the west and the east coasts. Telford's report was received with acclaim and he set out on what was to be his greatest achievement – the opening up of the Highlands to the modern age.

General Wade's military roads had mostly fallen into disrepair and Telford was critical of the way many of them took to extremely high ground, as in the case of the Corrieyairick Pass. Wade, of course, was neither architect nor engineer, but basically a military man.

Telford had assembled a team of experienced men who had worked with him in Wales, including John Mitchell, a skilled stonemason from Elgin, who was succeeded by his son Joseph. He was thus able to delegate work and to continue as consultant on various projects in England. By 1803 his great work on the Caledonian Canal was under way.

Telford's fame as an engineer had by this time spread not only nation-wide, but also to the Continent. In 1808 he received a letter from the King of Sweden asking for his consultation on the possibility of building a ship canal from the North Sea to the Baltic. Count von Platen was the instigator of the plan. Telford met him in Sweden. The two became friends and corresponded for many years. Telford sent several of his own engineers to Sweden to provide the necessary expertise.

The building of the Gotha Canal encountered the same problems as had that of the Caledonian Canal. It vastly exceeded the original estimate and took many years to complete. The Count, sadly, died three years before it was opened to shipping in 1832. Telford, by then, was 75 and in failing health. In 1992 a plaque was put up at Clachnaharry, at the eastern end of the Caledonian Canal, acknowledging Telford's work in the building of the Gotha Canal.

To return to the Highlands – in 1811-12 Telford built one of his most beautiful and graceful bridges, the Bonar Bridge, across the River Oykel in Sutherland. It was of cast iron and of so delicate a structure that a native of the area, it is recorded by Southey, said: 'As I went along, by the side of the water, I could see no bridge; at last I came in sight of something like a spider's web in the air ... oh it is the finest thing that ever was made by God or man.'

Robert Southey, Poet Laureate, met Telford about this time and took a great liking to him, recording: 'there is so much intelligence in his countenance, so much frankness, kindness and hilarity about him, flowing from the never-failing spring of a happy nature, that I was on cordial terms with him in five minutes.'

The two men travelled together through the Highlands for six weeks, Southey recording in his diary and his letters the improving conditions brought about by the building of the roads. Telford's love of poetry was an added factor in their mutual regard. On parting company Southey wrote of his friend: 'A man more heartily to be liked, more worthy to be esteemed and admired I have never fallen in with.' Thomas Telford it was who, in his speech of the Borders country, called the Great Glen 'this remarkable valley'.

Southey, in his diaries, gives quite detailed descriptions of Telford's road-building methods. He calls him, punningly, the 'Colossus of Roads' and also 'Pontifex Maximus'. Both these appellations are amazingly appropriate. During his preoccupation with the Caledonian and Gotha Canals he had been continuously in demand as consultant on roads and bridges in many parts of the country.

From 1821 a new form of communication was being mooted – the railway. As a promoter and builder of canals Telford's attitude to the railways was, understandably, not welcoming. Tramways had long been used for transporting materials to ongoing projects on roads, bridges or canals. Horse haulage had been the means of conveyance, not locomotive power. Telford advocated the use of the 'steam carriage', which did not run on costly fixed metal rails. This idea was tried out, but was killed when heavy tolls were imposed on the roads.

Canals had, of course, always posed problems. Tunnels had had to be dug, shafts made, reservoirs built. As the locomotive began to run at the 'novel speed of 12 miles an hour' it became evident that it was the railway which was going to satisfy the ever clamant demand by growing industries for faster means of communication.

Telford's last canal – the Birmingham and Liverpool junction canal – was an effort to meet that demand, but it encountered many difficulties and sadly he died, in 1834, before it was completed. Railway mania was now rampant.

During his busy years Telford had made his headquarters at the Salopian Coffee House at Charing Cross. At the age of 64 he at last acquired a house of his own in Abingdon Street, Westminster. This gave him real pleasure and he enjoyed entertaining his many friends and acquaintances. He also took in some young budding engineers whom he tutored.

In 1820 he became first president of the newly formed Institution of Civil Engineers. His portrait was painted by Raeburn. But, sadly, his last years were not entirely tranquil. Increasing deafness began to isolate him. He could no longer take part in the lively conversation he so much enjoyed. And certain rivals, envious of his achievements, began to disparage his success. He continued to read widely. He kept in touch with Eskdale, sending money to be distributed to kinsfolk and to be spent on libraries so that no one should be deprived of books. The poets Sothey and Campbell remained his friends. Despite his wish to be buried quietly, in the graveyard of his parish church, at the instigation of members of the Society of Civil Engineers, the nave of Westminster Abbey became his resting place. 25 years after his death, the body of the great railway engineer, Robert Stephenson, was, at his own request, laid beside that of Thomas Telford. A fitting tribute.

The Quiet Side

THE SOUTH SIDE of the loch is the quiet side, as the road which runs along the shore, with all its twists and turns, dips and climbs, is the old road, and has not been as fully developed for motor traffic as has its counterpart on the north. It was built by General Wade with detachments of soldiers as part of the plan to facilitate the movement of troops sent in to quell uprisings in the Highlands.

Wade's first road to link the forts of Inverness and Kilchumein (Fort Augustus), built in 1726, went over high ground to the south of Loch Ness. Winter conditions here made passage sometimes difficult. In 1732 the road along the shore of the loch was constructed. This involved some blasting of rock, walling and so on, but it was completed and is the basis of the tarred road of today.

On the western outskirts of Inverness is some good agricultural land; hedgerows hung with brambles in autumn and a canopy of trees. Further, just off the road to the right, stands the old house of Borlum, a typical 18th century laird's residence, built on the site of a medieval castle, the foundation stones still to be seen in the cellars. It was home to Mackintosh of Borlum, known as the 'Brigadier', a 'gallant old warrior' who had been involved in Jacobite activities since the end of the 17th century. He was captured in England, escaped, was exiled, then imprisoned again in Edinburgh. While in captivity there he wrote a treatise – *Essays on Ways and Means for Planting and Fallowing Scotland*. The centuries-old trees and square fields (square for easier cultivating), the results of his ideas, can be seen in the area today. He also wrote *A Scheme for curbing depradation in the Highlands*. His advocacy in this is only now being followed. He died aged 81 in 1743.

A stone circle in this area, near Crow Wood, is evidence of very early occupation. It is thought to have been a place of Druid worship. On high ground to the south, ground owned for generations by MacBains, the present chief, now living in America, has built a hillside memorial garden, with heather and shrubs. A path leads to the shelter of a wall, built of natural stone. A plaque here shows the history of the clan. In this quiet place a great vista of the loch and its surrounding hills stretches westward to the imagined sea.

A little further on the road westward we come to Aldourie School, a substantial building at the roadside. It stands on the site of an older parish school, which, according to a report in the papers of the Forfeited Estate Commissioners, was established in 1761. Provision of education was part of the government policy of 'civilising' the Highland people.

As far back as 1709 a Scottish Society for the Propagation of Christian Knowledge, known as the SSPCK, was set up, with a view to having schools run on Christian principles. The teachers were to be 'men of piety, loyalty, prudence, gravity, competent knowledge and literature and other Christian and necessary qualifications suited to their respective stations.'

In 1738, in a second patent, it was advocated that 'such of

the children as they shall think fit, to be instructed and bred up to husbandry and housewifery, or in trades and manufactures, or in such like manual occupations as the Society shall think proper.'

In 1777, the school, known then as Dores School, had 60 pupils with a teacher called John Forbes, who had an annual salary of £10. The teaching was in English, with children speaking in their native tongue, even in the playground, being severely punished. By 1787, however, some Gaelic learning had been introduced.

In 1825 Mr Davidson, the schoolmaster, was hoping that alterations would be made to the schoolhouse. In 1836, in the *Inverness Journal* of 17 June, an advertisement appeared for a 'Schoolmaster for the Parish of Dores, qualified to teach English, Reading and Grammar, Writing, Arithmetic, Geography, Mathematics, Latin and Greek. Knowledge of Church Music will be an additional recommendation. The salary is (besides free house and garden) £30 a year and the school fees may be as much more.'

The standard of education was high. In 1854, when two ministers examined the school, they found: 'the reading was accurate, the writing, arithmetic, geography and history such as would be held good in any of our chief towns; and all this while the schoolhouse is little else than a wooden shed and the salary of the enthusiastic teacher not equal to that of a day labourer.'

The local landowners, the Fraser-Tytlers, were supportive of the school, supplying books as prizes and treats for the children. The schoolmaster's wife taught the girls sewing and knitting, in return for a small salary.

After the Education Act of 1872, when schooling was made compulsory for children between the ages of five and 13, the headmaster was obliged to keep a log book, with entries recording the daily life of the school. These books give valued insights into the life of communities as a whole, as a form of social history.

It was at this time that schools, with a schoolhouse attached, were built, in solid Victorian style, all over the Highlands. Attendance at school being compulsory, officers were appointed to ensure that children did attend. Parents were reprimanded and occasionally fined for prolonged absences.

There was a large variation in the school roll at Dores over the years. In the 1880s it rose to over 70 and increased dramatically during the time of the Second World War when evacuee children arrived from the cities. Extra accommodation had to be provided for them in village halls. Many were found to be suffering from skin and other diseases.

After the war the roll dropped again and today stays at about 20 pupils. With a teacher in the modern mould the school is flourishing, with the children being helped to discover their heritage, not only linguistically but with outings to explore their environment with all its history and its folklore, as well as its geological foundations and its rich flora and fauna. The children speak happily in French!

The school garden has been awarded a notable prize as a habitat for wildlife and the school has lately celebrated its 125th birthday, with a weeklong event recording past times and ending with a céilidh. A book on the history of the school is in preparation.

On the right a road leads down to Aldourie Castle. This is the baronial style pile seen from the north side of the loch. The square tower is the oldest part of the building, dating from 1626. In about 1850 Colonel William Fraser-Tytler raised it by two storeys, added the stone turrets and put in a cement fireproof base between the ground and the first floor. This had the strange effect of laying to rest the ghost of a lady in grey that used to wander from the west bedroom to the front room. In 1903 a further wing was added with a dining room. Following the death of Colonel Cameron, the property has now been sold.

By the outer door stand two cannons from the galley that used to take supplies to the garrison at Fort Augustus in the 18th century. Here, also, are several beautiful decorated stone planters made at the local pottery. This was set up in 1900, by Mary, a member of the Fraser-Tytler family and the wife of the artist G.F. Watts, to give local employment. Houses were built for a manager and workers. The present village hall stands on the site of the old pottery. The clay was dug, initially, from a field in the area. Later, some was imported from the south. Sadly, many of the young workers were killed in the First World War and in 1920 the pottery was closed. Many beautiful pots were made – flowerpots, sundials – with the mark: 'Aldourie, Dores'.

In the grounds round the Castle are many fine specimen trees and shrubs. In spring the rhododendrons, azaleas and daffodils bring colour and grace to the whole area. Beyond Aldourie, at the lochside, is the former settlement of Bona. Drovers taking cattle from the north to markets in the south came ashore here.

Along the shore, westwards, are the remains of the pier, where steamers would call, and of the 'galley stance', a small inlet where the galleys were harboured. Some boat building was done at one time, the woodland providing much valuable material.

Until well into last century a barge, worked on a pulley, would operate here from a stance on Loch Dochfour. Heavy loads could be pulled over, even a horse and cart, or a household 'flitting'.

This saved a long journey round by Inverness. Rowing boats were also constantly ferrying people over. Care had to be taken to keep the small craft from getting washed over the nearby weir.

After the disruption in the Church of Scotland in 1843 people seeking a place to worship in the new way would make their way over the water and walk miles to the church of their choice. Still today is remembered the sound of the psalm singing wafting across the water, from the people in the small boats, on calm summer evenings.

Up a small incline to the south stands the old house of Clune. A tragic happening here is recorded in *Tales of old days on the Aldourie estate*:

Late in the evening after the battle of Culloden, a company of dragoons pulled up at the old house of Clune. What was the lady's horror when she recognised her husband's plaid on the shoulders of the officer in command. The plaid was said to have been of beautiful texture and to have had not only the Fraser crest on it, but also the words: '*Fear Chluain*' (the tacksman of Clune). She learnt from him that her husband had put up a desperate fight before he was cut down. It is said that the lady conducted herself with great calm and presence of mind. The troops then left, clearing the place of all livestock.

Dores

THE VILLAGE OF DORES – the name is said to be of Gaelic origin, meaning 'dark woods' – has grown over the last 1,500 years from a tiny chapel of the early Celtic church, probably built by a missionary of Saint Columba in the 6th century AD. It is likely that it was blessed by the saint himself, for he was active in the area. A fragment of a grave-slab carved in the Iona style was found on the beach nearby and was taken to the Museum of Antiquities in Edinburgh, now the National Museums of Scotland. The present church was built on the site of the early chapel.

Dr Thomas Sinton, a Gaelic scholar and local historian, who was minister at Dores from 1889–1923, called the place Kirktown, showing the importance of the church in the life of the settlement. In the graveyard can still be seen the 'watch-house', where, to guard against corpse lifting, men were stationed every night for about six weeks after each burial. Stories of the infamous activities of Burke and Hare, who sold corpses to the doctors at the Medical School in Edinburgh for dissection and study, had spread throughout the country, causing panic and horror. The men on 'watch' were provided liberally with refreshment and fuel, so that their duty was almost a convivial occasion.

Below the church stood the original inn and nearby was the meal-mill, so this area was very much the heart of the settlement. Later, the inn was at a place near the shore, at the junction of the road to Stratherrick, and became a 'King's House', that is, a lodging for troops on exercise. In the 19th century, if drink ran out, a smoke signal would bring the secret distillers over from Abriachan to replenish stocks. Today, the place is a very pleasant hostelry.

After their defeat at Culloden in April 1746, survivors of the Jacobite army made their way home by the lochside through Dores. Many died of their wounds and were buried beside the road, their graves marked by cairns, now overgrown. Prince Charles was also making his way west, on the higher ground to the south, at the start of his long summer in hiding in the hills.

Dr Sinton tells how the minister of Dores at the time, the Rev Archibald Bannatyne, though himself a Hanoverian, left out food – oatmeal and water – for the weary stragglers, even allowing some of them to shelter in his cellar, at great personal risk.

Dr Sinton collected stories of the time from James Smith, of Erchit Wood, known as 'James Gow', the blacksmith, whose grandfather had hidden in a cave to escape his pursuers after Culloden. Another man, Hugh Fraser of Foyers, nicknamed Bonaid Odhair (Grey Bonnet) also hid in a cave. A girl going up to his hiding place with food one day was followed by a soldier. Hugh, from his lookout, spotted the man and quickly shot him dead. Another time, a boy carrying beer was met by a party of soldiers. The cask fell from his shoulders. The men cut off his hand when he refused to reveal his master's whereabouts. Life was precarious for everyone.

In the 17th century some iron smelting was done in the area, using charcoal from the woodland. So, with some boat-building in the 18th century and, later, the pottery, Dores has been a busy place over the years. Shortly after the end of the First World

War a handsome archway into the graveyard of the parish church was erected as a memorial to the men of the district who lost their lives in the war. Mrs Watts, who ran the pottery at Dores, designed the archway. Panels on the front, in a design called 'the garment of praise', had a symbolical meaning, the names of the men who were killed on two tablets below. The sculpture was done in the pottery. Sadly, it has not survived, but the archway stands firm. General Sandilands performed the unveiling ceremony. A large gathering of people then joined in a service of prayer and praise led by local clergy.

Today, after the building of council houses, Dores has become almost a dormitory town for workers in Inverness, some 10 miles distant. But it is still very much a lochside place. New developments include a fish farm a few miles along the loch and water-skiing in the sheltered bay. The pebble beach is a pleasant place on a summer day. Ducks and swans swim close in-shore. In really hot weather, a few hardy people join them. One or two of these, well greased and wet-suited, have been known to swim across from the old pier at Abriachan and have survived to tell the tale!

In a caravan nearby a man has lived for several years, keeping almost continuous watch for any unusual creatures in the loch. So far, results have not been promising, but his patience is still strong.

Leaving Dores by the lochside road, the village hall can be seen, on the left, on the site of the former pottery. Scraps of the 'Aldourie' ware are still sometimes unearthed. High above the road, sturdy ropes link pine-trees on the upside to hazels by the shore, making safe walkways for the red squirrels, linking their nest-sites to their feeding-grounds, thus affording protection for this endangered species.

Further west, in the bank on the up-side of the road, two wells still flow. Their names can be made out, carved into the stone, though somewhat obscured by moss. One is the Well of the Phantom Hand. Ghostly fingers must, once or twice, have been seen scooping up a drink to ghostly lips! A little further on is the General's Well, where General Wade would quench his thirst on a warm day's road-building.

On the flat ground by the loch his soldiers, whom he called his 'Highwaymen', had their huts. A path along the loch shore leads through woodland to the site of the old 'Change House', that is, the inn where fresh carriage horses were available, in exchange for those tired by the journey from Inverness. The outlines of several buildings can be made out – the inn itself, the stables, and also a small house where an old woman was done to death by Hanoverian soldiers who tried, unsuccessfully, to kidnap her granddaughter.

An account of a sighting of a strange creature in this area, some 100 years ago, has been recorded. It concerns a young man and his father, thus:

On his way home to Foyers with his father, they were just two miles north of Inverfarigaig when their pony suddenly stopped and began backing away in fright. He said it very nearly backed them off the road and down the bank. Then something very large crossed the road about 20 yards ahead of them. It had come out of the trees above the road and moved very slowly across it, down the bank and, as they heard a splash they presumed it went into the water. It was seemingly too dark and they were too busy controlling the pony to notice any other detail, other than it was a big beast, fully the width of the road. He remembers his father muttering something in Gaelic, hurried home and never mentioned the incident again.

Near where this 'sighting' took place is the old bridge over the river Farigaig, built by the general. It was still in use until quite recently, when the increased volume of traffic caused some up-grading of the road. From the small settlement of Inverfarigaig, where the river joins the loch, a road leads up to hill ground. A short way up, on a rock face, is an inscription:

In memory of James Bryce, LLD, FGS, FRSE, a distinguished geologist, born near Coleraine, Ireland, in 1806, killed oppo-site this spot, while in pursuit of his favourite science, July 11, 1877. Erected by scientific friends in Edinburgh, Glasgow and Inverness.

In 1883 a member of his family presented James Bryce's mineral collection to the Inverness Scientific Society and Field Club. It is now in the Museum in Inverness. Scientists in the 19th century were passionately interested in geology and often risked their lives in studying rocks in the Highlands. Many were inspired by the writings of Hugh Miller, the stonemason turned geologist, from Cromarty.

Further up this road is an Interpretation Centre run by Forest Enterprise, where information about the trees, plants, birds, animals, rocks to be found in the area is attractively displayed, with modern technology. Here are the remains of ancient wood-land and many paths lead through the trees. It is possible to scram-ble up to Dun Dearduil, an Iron Age fort, said to have been the refuge of 'Deirdre of the Sorrows'. She escaped the clutches of

King Conacher, who wished to marry her, and fled Ireland with her lover to spend some happy years in exile. According to Irish legend 'they settled and made a dwelling-house for themselves by the side of Loch Ness, and they could kill the salmon of the stream from out of their own door and the deer of the grey hills out of their window.'

Along the shore here are the remains of several small piers, in use when the loch was a busy shipping lane. Juniper bushes are plentiful. In the 19th century a flourishing export trade in berries to Holland brought in some welcome cash. In earlier times the loch had been used for the export of timber. Pine and oak were floated down to Inverness. In 1249 a ship was built there by the Earl of St Pol & Blois to take him and his followers to the Holy Land. In 1563 one William Fraser blocked the passage of Loch Ness on account of 'damage done to woods by peeling, cutting, green timber and bark going to Inverness'. The bark was used in the tanning trade.

A large churchyard just below the road at Boleskine contains the scant remains of an early chapel, later made into a mausoleum for members of the Fraser clan. One day, not long after the Battle of Culloden, when a burial was taking place, a party of soldiers, with a wagonload of supplies for the garrison at Fort Augustus, went past on the nearby road. One of the mourners seized a loaf of bread from the wagon and, to show his contempt, threw it to a dog. The soldiers fired a volley. The bullet marks are still visible on the headstone of Donald Fraser of Erchit. One man was arrested and taken to the fort. The local minister, for whom the occupying authority had some respect, later managed to get this prisoner released.

On the bullet-marked stone is an inscription:

A flower most bright, both pleasant and compleat
Is in the grave, from ills now laid asleep,
O cruel death, will neither youth nor age
Nor grace nor virtue stop thy chariots.

1730

Donald Fraser died aged 27 – a real tragedy.

Another interesting inscription also tells a story. It reads: 'Stone in memory of James Anderson from Northumberland who died at Garthmore 1811.' He would probably have been one of the shepherds brought in by the new flockmasters from the South. James Gow is also buried here. He died in 1903 at the age of 100.

Boleskine House, which stands on higher ground above the graveyard, was once the home of Aleister Crowley, known as 'the wickedest man in the world', and the 'Great Beast' of black magic. Born in 1875 into a family of Plymouth Brethren, he had an unhappy early life, being bullied at boarding school. He later found release in learning to become an accomplished Alpine climber. He was 'a rebel against the stifling conformity of the Victorian age and against the religious extremism of his early upbringing.' He made the acquaintance of several well-known writers – Somerset Maugham, Arnold Bennett, W.B. Yeats – and wrote poems, short stories and novels, also *The Confessions*, an autobiography. He married, but, sadly, lost both wife and child to illness. Prescribed heroin for asthma, he became an addict. Taking as his motto 'Do what thou wilt', he established a commune in Sicily, where licentious behaviour at that time was tolerated, from which he was later expelled.

Behaviour of a somewhat similar kind was indulged in during

his time at Boleskine, 1900–1918. He was, in fact, a forerunner of the hippie generation and was admired by many of them. The local people were not sure what to make of him. He had three dogs – a great dane, an alsatian and a bulldog. He was inclined to live the life of a laird at Boleskine, going climbing, fishing and shooting. He had a ghillie and a piper, of whom he thought the world. He wrote: 'much to my disgust commercialism thrust its ugly head into my neighbourhood.' The British Aluminium Company proposed to exploit the waterpower of the valley above Foyers. His housekeeper, 'unable to bear the eerieness of the place', disappeared, his coachman took to drink, and one worker went mad and tried to kill him. The *enfant terrible* of the Victorian age, he ended his life in poverty, but with the companionship of one woman who admired him. The house was later taken over by the group known as Led Zeppelin. It is now in private – and quiet – hands.

Droving

IN THE DAYS when motor cars were few and far between, most vehicles using real horse power, cattle would be driven on the roads along Loch Ness to a market in Inverness. Sometimes they would be shod, as a road was hard on their feet. Boys would take a day off school to keep the beasts from wandering through the open doors of shops in the high street! Today they arrive in huge lorries, their frightened eyes peering through ventilation slots.

It was in the time before the advent of the railway train, with its huge cattle trucks, that the drovers took their beasts on the grassy hill tracks to the lucrative markets of the south. With their livelihoods on the hoof in front of them, moving through the hazards of the route, they had an anxious time of it.

Until the breakdown of the clan society in the 17th century it was expected of a young chief that he would make a raid on his neighbours' cattle as proof of his manhood. If he carried off a *spreidh* of beasts he knew quite well that his neighbour would retaliate. This was an aristocratic pursuit said to date back to an ancient Indo-European custom. Cattle were wealth in a real sense. The main Highland festivals were Beltane, the first of May, when the cattle were driven up to the high pastures – the shieling grounds – and Samhain, the first of November, when they were returned to their winter quarters near the settlements.

Members of some more settled clans profited by keeping watch in the glens through which the raiders passed. When a *spreidh* was driven through lands belonging to another clan, even a friendly one, a share of the booty was demanded.

With lawless times changing and a money economy creeping in, cattle became looked on not only as sustainers of life, providing meat, milk, clothing, but also as products which could be bought and sold for cash and used to provide other goods. Commercialisa-tion had arrived.

'Trysts', market-places for the buyers and sellers, were set up at Muir-of-Ord, near Inverness, at Crieff in Perthshire, and as far south as Falkirk, to catch the English trade, the drovers travelling hundreds of miles. Perhaps the best known of the drove roads is the one going from Fort Augustus to Speyside by the Corrieyairick. It was one of those which General Wade upgraded.

The trysts were busy places. As well as the drovers there were dealers, with a practised eye for a good beast, auctioneers, peddlers shouting their wares, beggars and entertainers, jugglers and singers. It was a motley crowd, Gaelic, Scots and English speakers haggling, arguing, joking, sometimes coming to blows.

The drovers enjoyed their days at the trysts, or 'fairs' as they were known, exchanging news and gossip and getting a glimpse of the wider world. The church could be disapproving, as the fairs often coincided with saints' days and Sunday was not a time for dealing in marketing affairs.

Droving from the Highlands took place during the summer months when the hours of daylight were long. It could be a hazardous journey, with the ever-present fear of marauders lying in wait, summer storms never far away and cold nights, even in July.

Droves might be of up to 300 beasts, with a drover to every

50 or 60. They covered about 12 miles a day. Cattle were afraid of crossing bridges, preferring to use fords. In the face of any problem a drover would take a dozen or so beasts ahead, which the others would follow. Cattle coming from Skye would be swum over the narrows at Kylerhea. Those coming from the north would also be swum over at Bona, at the east end of Loch Ness. The building of new roads which was taking place during the 18th and 19th centuries meant that cattle were sometimes shod, like horses, with metal plates. Smithies were set up at various points for the repairing of shoes.

The drovers were careful not to press the cattle hard. Some drovers still living in the early 20th century remembered their droving days.

> They [the cattle] were in full bloom and full of flesh and hair. If you sweated them the hair dropped and never got up again into the same condition. The great secret was to take them there as good-looking as they were when they left home. One would think there was nothing but drive and force them on with a stick, but that wasn't allowed at all. They'd go quite nicely, when they were left alone.

A halt would be made at mid-day, at familiar resting places, when the cattle would graze and get a drink. At night a watch was kept on the herd as some beasts, obeying instinct, would try to make for home. There was also the ever-present fear of raiders.

On one known occasion a small drove was carried off by men lying in wait and the few drovers killed. Mostly, the drovers walked barefoot. As a Skye bard put it (in Gaelic):

Often did they go to Falkirk
Driving cattle through the rough mountains
And no shoe went on their feet
Until they returned to the Mist which they had left behind.

They carried food: oatmeal with onions, cheese and bannocks, with a ram's horn of whisky. Often they had to eat the oatmeal mixed with cold water, if a fire could not be made. Occasionally they would resort to bleeding a beast, mixing the oatmeal with warm blood. At night they slept on the ground, wrapped in their plaids, waking early to shake off the dew or the frost.

Certain well-known stopping places such as the green at Drumnadrochit, where the drovers from the west rested their cattle overnight, became known as stances. There was no charge for this overnight accommodation, as the manuring was valued. In later times, when road-tolls were introduced, some payment had to be made.

Occasionally the drovers would stop with a shepherd or gamekeeper known to them. They seldom stayed at an inn, though Dorothy Wordsworth, writing in her journal in 1803, found Kingshouse, on the moor of Rannoch, 'filled with seven or eight travellers, probably drovers sitting in a complete circle round a large peat fire in the middle of the floor, each with a mess of porridge in a wooden vessel on his knee.'

The drovers had to be hardy men. Some would take home-made goods – wooden dishes, horn spoons – for sale at the trysts. Some were even known to knit stockings as they walked. There were bards among them, too, who found the long days in the hills and glens a time for composition. Rob Donn, the famous poet from Sutherland, went often to the trysts.

The drovers were exempt from the Disarming Acts of 1716 and 1746, imposed after the Jacobite uprisings. They could carry a gun, a sword and a pistol. This was essential, with the fear of raiders on the outward journey and on their return when it was known they would be carrying cash. Sometimes they turned the cash into silver buttons which could be hidden and sold on arrival home. The dogs they took with them would often be sent home on their own, sure instinct reminding them where they would find food and a welcome, as they had on the way down.

Rob Roy MacGregor was a drover in his day. Always keen to improve his lot he worked a system of 'blackmail', a kind of insurance against the theft of cattle. Cattle of course could be lost in other ways, through accident, disease, delays on the road. Eventually, Rob Roy reverted to his old ploy of cattle raiding and became well known as an outlaw.

Perhaps the most famous drover was John Cameron of Corrychoille, from Kilmonivaig in Lochaber, who lived from 1780 to 1856. He had a hard life of it but eventually had many farms, some 20,000 sheep and several thousand cattle. Joseph Mitchell, the engineer, describes him thus:

> He was a badly dressed little man, about 5 ft 6 ins in height, of thin make, with a sharp, hooked nose and lynx eyes. A man of great energy, he frequently rode night and day, on a wiry pony, from Falkirk to the Muir of Ord, 120 miles, carrying for himself some bread and cheese in his pocket and giving his pony now and again a bottle of porter . . . he did not die a rich man.

The Loch Ness area would have seen a lot of the drovers. As well as those coming from the west to the stance at

Drumnadrochit before going over the Corrieyairick pass, there would have been many from the north swimming their cattle over the river Ness at Bona. They would have been welcomed as bringers of news from other parts and some would no doubt have been given shelter or food.

Many of the old drove roads can be walked today. Some have been signposted as 'pathways', with distances indicated. They lead into some of the most beautiful parts of the Highlands, through glens and over high moorland. Walking them without cattle is pure enjoyment!

Some Frasers of
Loch Ness Country

THE FRASERS WHO became Lords of Lovat had their original domain well to the north of Loch Ness, in the country known as the Aird, the 'high ground', and west into Strathfarrar. It is thought that the family came from Anjou and Normandy, as part of the Norman invasion of the eleventh century. The Fraser arms are silver strawberry flowers on a field of blue, the French for strawberry being *fraise*, from which the surname derives, although it is not known for certain how this name came to be applied to this family. Did they have a liking for this particular fruit? Did they grow it in large quantities? It is certainly a plant that grows well in Highland soil. The Gaelic for the name is *Friseil*, leading to one of its variant versions in English, Frisel. The Fraser motto is *je suis prest*, Norman French for 'I am ready'. The Frasers were first in Scotland in 1160, when a Simon Fraser made the gift of a church to the monks of Kelso Abbey. During the 12th and 13th centuries they moved north.

Another Simon Fraser was captured fighting for Robert the Bruce and executed with great cruelty by Edward I in 1306. His family received lands by Scots royal charter. A Hugh Fraser was styled 'of Lovat' ('Lovat' meaning swampy ground) as, through marriage, he had acquired lands formerly held by the Byssets, another powerful in-comer family, in the Beauly area. In 1422 Hugh was confirmed in possession of extensive lands in the area to the south of Loch Ness known as Stratherrick.

The Frasers flourished in the lands here, to which they became particularly attached, sons and grandsons, the 'cadets' of the families, being given their shares in the area. The ground was not overly fruitful, but it certainly bred a race of fighting men. This was vitally important when the power of a clan chief lay in the numbers he could count on to support him in combat. By now the head of the Fraser family had become such a clan chief. The rallying point for the Frasers of Stratherrick was at the Fraser Yew, a huge tree on the shore of Loch Ness at Knockie, towards the western end of the loch. From this tree they cut their bows and drew their clan badge – a sprig of yew.

In 1499 Hugh, a natural son of Lord Fraser of Lovat, received a charter from his father for the lands of Foyers, on Loch Ness. These had formerly been in the possession of the Grants, another Anglo-Norman family, who had lost them in a dramatic fashion in the early 1400s. The new wife of a MacGruer, from the north side of the loch, was on a visit to friends, as was the custom, when Laurence Grant insulted her. Her husband, to avenge her, set out across the loch with several boats full of fighting men. Grant, with his men, sailed out to meet him and a battle ensued. Eventually, Grant was defeated, taken across the loch and killed. MacGruer then took over the lands of Foyers. His descendants are still in the area. There are also MacGillivrays, MacTavishes and others.

The Hugh Fraser who was in possession of Foyers in 1499 was known as Uisdean Frangach, 'French Hugh', on account of his having spent a number of years exiled in France after being accused of murdering a half-brother. Eventually he came home, bringing with him a French wife. The romantic story is that, staying one night in a lonely inn, he heard a girl singing a child to sleep. As he listened he heard her insert into the song a verse warning him of danger. Immediately he made his escape, taking the girl with him.

French Hugh was a man of frank disposition and a lover of manly sports. Descendants of his remained in the area of Foyers for many years. They were known as spirited men, like himself, and famed for their hospitality. The last of the line, Simon Fraser, is buried, with his wife, beside the grave of his only child, Jane, in a quiet place overlooking Loch Ness.

Captain Simon Fraser of Knockie kept alive the tradition of music and song in the country. His father, Captain John, had been a well-known piper and singer and an authority on Highland music. In 1816 Simon published *The Airs and Melodies peculiar to the highlands of Scotland and the Isles*. It is still studied by students of the bagpipe today.

The Frasers never shirked from a fight. In 1514, in a battle with the Macdonalds over the chieftainship of that clan, Frasers from Stratherrick must have been among the 300 slain. There were Frasers of Erchite, of Boleskine, of Errogie, of Farraline and of other parts. The battle, known as the Battle of Blar-na-leine (the field of the shirt), was fought on a hot summer day; so hot that the combatants discarded their heavy clothing and stripped to their shirts, tying them between their legs to make movement easier in the wild hand-to-hand fighting that ensued. Discharging their arrows, they abandoned their bows and charged the foe with sword and axe. Only one Fraser survived the battle. Carried from the field by a faithful servant, he died soon afterwards. Decimation of the clan was enormous. Fortunately, however, many wives of the young clansmen were pregnant at the time, so that numbers gradually increased again.

Some 200 years later, when times were hard and emigration was in the air, an effort was made to prevent further loss. Families of different origins were invited to join the clan with the offer of protection and sustenance. Those who accepted became known as 'boll o' meal' Frasers.

In the later 18th century, when many men were enlisting in the army, the 78th Regiment, Fraser's Highlanders, fought the French in North America, some taking part in General Wolfe's famous victory at Quebec. Some Frasers were subsequently given land in Canada.

During the Boer War, in 1900, Simon Fraser, Lord Lovat, raised the Lovat Scouts, many Frasers distinguishing themselves then and subsequently. In the Second World War, Simon Fraser, the next Lord Lovat, was the outstanding Commando officer who led many Frasers into enemy-occupied lands – the fighting instinct never abated.

James Fraser, Church of Scotland minister at Wardlaw, Kirkhill, in Lovat Fraser country, wrote a very full and learned history of the clan, with all its branches – *Genealogy of the Frasers 916–1674* – which can be read with great interest today.

Raising a Regiment

COMBAT HAD ALWAYS been a part of life for the Highlander. Clan loyalty had meant an instinctive response to the call-to-arms. In the late 18th century when the traditional clan life was waning, young men were encouraged to join the army. Many did, as this, at least, meant they were assured of sustenance and, better still, the feel of a weapon in their hands again, and even the sound of the pipes. Their bravery was highly prized in Britain's Continental and American wars.

In the late 19th century, Britain was fighting the Boers – Dutch farmers in South Africa – and things were going badly for the British. It seemed that they had not got the measure of the enemy; were not familiar with his fighting ways.

After one particularly bad defeat, at Maggersfontein in 1899, Simon Joseph Fraser, Lord Lovat, suggested to the War Office that a body of Highlanders could be assembled, as were the 'Fencibles' at the time of the Napoleonic wars, given some basic training and sent to South Africa, to defeat the Boers at their own game. As countrymen, their natural ability in stalking, shooting, spying out the land, would make them skilled in guerrilla tactics, he argued. The War Office people were at first sceptical, but eventually agreed to give the idea a try.

In a letter dated 4 January 1900, sent to all Highland landowners, Lord Lovat said:

I have been asked by the War Office to raise a corps of 150 stalkers, ghillies and picked men for primarily scouting service in South Africa... As it is essential to secure the best stamp of man with all possible dispatch I would be much obliged if you could see your way to send for some of the most likely men in your district and acquaint them with the scheme, in order that they may have both an opportunity of judging for themselves, and also of acquainting others of what is on foot.

The men were to enlist for one year, their pay, allowances and bounties the same as for men on active service. They were to be attached to the Black Watch and to be commanded by Highland officers.

Men from both sides of Loch Ness, from Stratherrick, Glen Urquhart, Glen Moriston, Abriachan, from every area, joined up and within weeks a corps was mobilised at Beaufort. The men were billeted in the home farm, the officers, who were all local landowners, in the castle. As in former times, when chiefs and clansmen were close, the bonds between officers and men were those of friendly respect.

The Scouts, now known as Lovat's Scouts, were akin to the old clan regiments. They were kitted out in homespun tweed, with slouch hats sporting a red Fraser tartan flash. They were mounted, many men supplying their own garrons, the hardy workhorses found on most crofts. Shoeing-smiths and other craftsmen were recruited into the contingent and within the year they were on their way to South Africa. In the press there was some adverse criticism of the project, but in the field the men's skills were quickly recognised. Soon a second contingent was sent out. This included six shepherds who took their dogs with the idea of rounding up and impounding the Boers' cattle and sheep.

Sometimes there were problems with communication. For most of the men English was a second language acquired painfully at school and then mostly forgotten. Their thinking and speaking was, naturally, in Gaelic. The tactics they were to employ in the field – scouting, observing, stalking, shooting, signalling – suited them admirably, but the transmission of information to their, for the most part, English-speaking officers sometimes proved difficult.

Some unorthodoxy was smiled upon as their integrity and courage were recognised. General Hector Macdonald, himself the son of a crofting family, under whose command they came, said of them: 'As Scouts or Guides, on pony or on foot, as individual marksmen or as a collective body in the firing line, they are all specialists and picked men. They are a splendid band of Scotsmen, which is the highest compliment I can pay them.'

After the end of the Boer War recruiting to the Scouts continued. Training camps were organised. Pipers were welcome and were given kilts and hose of Fraser tartan. With the outbreak of war in 1914 a third contingent of about 1,200 Scouts was mobilised and was soon in action. They served at Gallipoli and there met the Gurkhas, those mountain men with whom they felt much affinity. Then, becoming infantrymen and loath to part with their mounts, they had to adapt to fighting in North Africa.

After the war they were mounted again and in 1939 were sent to Norway, then the following year to the Faroe Islands. The Faroese called them 'the best foreigners we ever met'. Several of them married Faroese women and they have kept a connection with the islands over the years. By this time the Pipe band, under their Pipe Major Donald Riddell, from Abriachan, had become the pride and joy of the Scouts.

After their spell in the Faroes they were sent to Canada for training in mountain warfare, including the use of skis. Here, to their delight, they came across some Canadians who still spoke the old Gaelic of their forebears. Then, in the Apennines, they again found extremely compatible allies in the Gurkhas. In an article in the *Inverness Courier* of the time the Scouts are described as 'McGurkhas'!

After the war they continued to attend training camps, becoming, in 1947, part of the Territorial Army, then re-designated a mountain regiment, serving in anti-aircraft. After the reorganisation of the Territorial Army in 1967, the Lovat Scouts, as such, were disbanded, although their legend lives on.

Foyers

THE HOTEL AT Foyers stands on the site of the former inn, known as the 'General's Hut', a modest place where General Wade would take his meals in road-building days. The village is in two parts, upper Foyers, where an attractive green is surrounded by former workers' houses, now modernised and sold to incomers, and lower Foyers, near the loch shore, where there are older workers' houses and the buildings of the old aluminium works. These are sound and beautiful structures. The great attraction of the place is in the falls. A path leads down through woodland to a view-point from which they can be seen to great advantage. Though the volume of water is less now than when the flow was in its original state, yet the falls are still spectacular and attract visitors from all over the world.

The southern shore of Loch Ness is perhaps the last place in which to expect industrial development, but that is exactly what happened in 1895, when the British Aluminium Company set up works there for the smelting of aluminium, derived from the ore known as bauxite. The bauxite was imported from Ireland, brought in along the Caledonian Canal. The electrical power needed for the process was supplied by the great force of water in the falls. Lord Kelvin, a famous scientist of the time, was advisor to the project. The work involved damming and sluicing the river above. The pipes are still in use today.

The scheme did not go ahead without a considerable amount of protest. In 1895 the National Trust for Places of Historic Interest and Natural Beauty sent a petition couched in strong terms against the despoiling of this place famed for its magnificence. A 'memorial' on the subject, signed by many well-known people, was also sent to Lord Balfour of Burleigh, Secretary for Scotland. John Ruskin and several others in the world of the arts added their names to the protesters. Robert Burns and Walter Scott had praised the beauty of the falls. Members of the Inverness Scientific Society also expressed concern, visiting the proposed site to consider the impact that this pioneering work would have.

In the *New Statistical Account of Scotland*, published in 1831, the falls are described thus:

> the large stones in the channel of the river over which the waters roll and foam, the weeping birch lining the precipitous banks at irregular intervals, the projecting misshapen rocks overhanging the tremendous gulf and the impetuous torrent below form a scene that cannot be beheld without admiration and awe.

Robert Burns, during his visit in 1787, had been so impressed by the grandeur of the falls that he wrote a poem, in pencil, on the spot.

Among the heathy hills and rugged woods,
The foaming Foyers pours his mossy floods
Till full he dashes on the rocky mounds
Where through a shapeless breach his stream resounds
As high in air the bursting torrents flow

As deep recoiling surges down below.
Prone down the rock the whitening sheet descends
And viewless Echo's ear astonished rends.
Dim seen thru' rising mist and ceaseless showers
The hoary cavern wide resounding low'rs.
Still thru' the gap the struggling river toils
And still below the horrid cauldron boils.

The lower fall is known in Gaelic as 'the fall of smoke'. In spite of protests the project to use the water for industrial purposes went ahead, the works were established, the river dammed and sluiced and by 1904 the output had risen to 1,000 tons of aluminium per year. During the two World Wars some 500 men were employed. Workers came from many parts of the country and from Ireland, Wales and the Hebrides. Joiners, builders, slaters, plumbers, electricians, painters, sawyers, welders, furnace men, all found welcome employment on the scheme. For these people houses were built, many of which still stand, a school and a church were opened and a resident doctor was employed. Some families worked for several generations at the plant.

In February 1941, a German plane came in from the North Sea, flew down the canal, made for Foyers and, at midday, aimed two huge bombs at the factory. An eyewitness said: 'It was a lovely day. One bomb struck the coping-stone of the power station and went into the hillside, fracturing pipes carrying water to the turbines. The second bomb fell in open ground. The pilot circled the area, flying very low above the school and waved to children in the playground.' The explosion killed two men. Partial production was restarted the following day and repairs were completed within a few weeks.

In 1954 the plant was converted to produce 'super purity' aluminium. Foyers was the 'cradle of the industry', but by 1967 economic factors worldwide led to the closure of the works. Some 10 years later the North of Scotland Hydro-Electricity Board converted it into a reversible pumped storage station for the production of electric power. The original pipes bringing the river water down were still in use and water from Loch Ness was pumped up.

Some of the old buildings are now listed as constructions of great architectural merit. A boat-builder, son of an original worker, makes use of some smaller units and another local man has a salmon hatchery nearby.

To mark the centenary of the establishment of the aluminium works in 1895 a memorial stone was set up at the entrance to the walkways leading through the woodland to the different views of the falls. Though their power is diminished owing to their use in providing electricity, they are still spectacular, particularly after heavy rainfall. The setting of rock and forest is superb.

Through the graveyard at lower Foyers a path leads to a memorial stone, known only to a few. It is a marble slab, decorated with heraldic and symbolic figures and inscribed:

Sacred to the memory of Jane, spouse of Thomas Fraser of Balnain. She was the only child of Simon Fraser of Foyers and of Elizabeth Grant, his spouse. She added to superior personal grace and talents of the first order, the humblest piety, the sweetest temper and the most devoted filial affection. Her spotless life was closed by a tranquil and Christian death, on the 7th of July, 1817, in the 22nd year of her age.

The memorial was erected by Mrs Anne Grant of Laggan, with whom Jane had been staying in Edinburgh in order to pursue her studies. On the journey home from Edinburgh to the Highlands she was caught in a heavy snowstorm, having to walk a considerable distance after the carriage broke down in drifts. Badly chilled, she became ill and did not recover. The memorial stands in a place much loved by Jane, close to the shore, from where she would look over the loch to the home at Invermoriston of her first love, her cousin, Patrick Grant, who, sadly, died after a fall. She subsequently married Thomas Fraser. Jane's mother and father are buried close beside her, her father the last of the Frasers of Foyers.

The Road to the Fort

LEAVING FOYERS, the road takes us inland, away from the loch. Edmund Burt, the engineer, who was overseeing the building of roads and bridges with General Wade, in his book *Letters from the North of Scotland*, published in 1754, describing the road along Loch Ness, wrote:

> It is, good part of it, made out of rocks as hard as marble. There, the miners hung by ropes from the precipice over the water ... to bore the stone, in order to blow away a necessary part from the face of it, and the rest likewise was chiefly done by gunpowder, but, when any part of it was fit to be left as it was, being flat and smooth, it was brought to a roughness proper for a stay to the feet, and, in this part, and in all the rest of the road, where the precipices were like to give horror or uneasiness to such as might pass over them in carriages, though at a good distance from them, they are secured to the lakeside by walls, either left in the working or built up with stone, to a height proportioned to the occasion.

Burt goes on to describe a nuisance which the soldiers working on the road had to suffer and which people in many areas have to suffer today. He says:

I have been sometimes vexed with a little Plague (if I may use the expression). There are great swarms of little flies which the Natives call Malhousakins. Houlak, they tell me, signifies, in the country language, a fly and Houlakin is the Diminutive of that Name. These are so very small that separately, they are but just perceptible and that is all; and, being of a blackish colour, when a number of them settle on the skin, they make it look as if it was dirty; there, they soon bore with their little Augers, into the Pores and change the face from black to red. They are only troublesome (I should say intolerable) in Summer, when there is a profound Calm; for the least Breath of Wind immediately disperses them, and the only Refuge from them is the House, into which I never knew them to enter.

That is as good a description of the Midge and its modus operandi as any in more modern style!

Wade's enterprise took his Highwaymen away from the precipices near the loch. He always preferred working on high ground, often following the line of the old drove roads. To build a road along the loch shore here would have been an impossible task. Apart from two small piers where fishers may draw in their boats, the area remains almost inaccessible, rock, precipice, scree ensuring that it stays in its pristine state. The 'Horseshoe Crag', best seen from the other side of the loch, is here. Native trees, scrub, plants make it a small chunk of paradise for wildlife, and its caves have given shelter to hardy renegades.

For travellers using wheeled vehicles the way now goes uphill, proceeds with many twists and turns, till level ground is reached at the confluence of two rivers flowing from hill lochs. There is a small settlement known as Whitebridge, from the bridge built at the meeting of their waters. Still solid, though no longer in use, it stands there, a single arched, hump backed bridge, its graceful lines a testimony to the skill and strength of the designers, masons, labourers of the day. It was actually built by General Caulfield, an overseer who worked closely with Wade. The date 1732 is inscribed on the parapet. The hotel at White-bridge stands on the site of the former King's House, a hostelry no doubt frequented by the officers of the building squad.

A long, straight stretch of road, rising to between 200 and 300 metres, affords magnificent views of the surrounding hill-land, till it descends by Glen Doe to Loch Tarff. This loch, with its small wooded islands, not grazed by sheep or deer, is a place favoured by water birds of many kinds; mallard and tufted duck in winter, merganser, pochard and goldeneye in spring. Heron, and that lovely little fisher and singer, the dipper, are also around. The best form of 'hide' is probably a seat in a car, drawn up in a lay-by close to the shore.

A mile or so further on another bridge built in Wade's time can be seen. It is now by-passed by the modern road, which leads directly to Fort Augustus.

Summertime at the Shielings

THERE WERE MANY shielings on the high ground above Loch Ness. In the Highlands up to the 19th century, cattle were the mainstay of people's lives and keeping them in good heart was the object of most of the year's work. The glen leading up from Fort Augustus to the start of the Corrieyairick pass was known as the 'Dairy Glade'. At the shielings here the women and girls made butter and cheese which they stored in tubs buried in the peat.

In early summer, when the crops of oats, hay and potatoes were established in the low-ground fields and the peats for winter fuel were cut, the cattle would be driven up to the high pastures – the shielings – to feed and fatten on the sweet hill grass.

The women and girls, the children and the young men would go with them, the older men staying behind to look after the crofts. If the winter had been long and their food of hay and oat straw had almost given out, the cattle would be so weak that they would have to be lifted bodily from their stalls in spring. But some days of fresh grazing soon restored them sufficiently for the journey.

As the time for the departure drew near, there was always great excitement in the community. First came the 'small flitting', when the men would go up to repair the summer dwellings which might have been storm-damaged over the winter. They were simple structures, stone-walled with roofs of branches and heather thatch. There would be several of these little 'houses', one set aside for the milk vessels, away from the heat of the cooking fire. In some places the dwellings were of the old bee-hive style or built like tepees.

When everything in the way of repairs was seen to, it was time for the 'big flitting'. On the eve of departure, a feast of sorts was held, a simple meal taken in common with a blessing invoked in song on the cattle to ensure their well being.

One such song from Alexander Carmichael's collection *Carmina Gadelica* is known as *Columba's Herding* –

May the herding of Columba
Encompass you going and returning
Encompass you in strath and on ridge
And on the edge of each rough region
May it keep you from hill and from crag,
Keep you from loch and from downfall,
Each evening and each darkling.
The peace of Columba be yours in the grazing,
The peace of Brigit be yours in the grazing,
The peace of Mary be yours in the grazing,
And may you return home safe-guarded.

Then it was off, with the excited children laughing and shouting, dogs barking, the cattle lowing, the women casting anxious eyes on the loaded carts lest anything should be forgotten. Loaded they were with milk vessels, butter churns, cheese presses, pots, pans, meal-bags, salt-boxes, spinning wheels, spindles, flax, wool, blankets and clothing.

Some shielings were quite a distance from the crofts, some comparatively near. A few were known by the names of saints and they might have been places of retreat in the days of the early Celtic church. In most cases, the trek would take the best part of a day. Then came the unloading and the settling in. The men at the 'first flitting' would have cut and stacked some peat and gathered heather for the bedding. A fine springy bed the heather makes! There would be a simple, homemade table and seats with planks for shelves to hold the dairying equipment in the 'dairy' house. The women would get busy right away for milking cannot wait. The milking was done on the green near the dwelling, often with the cow's back legs tied together to keep her steady. The girls would have favourites among the cows, giving them names, knowing their individual ways and singing to them as they drew the milk, thus –

> Lovely black cow, pride of the shieling,
> First cow of the byre, choice mother of calves,
> Wisps of straw round the cows of the townland,
> As hackle of silk on my heifer beloved,
> Ho, my heifer, ho my gentle heifer.

Goats would be milked too and sometimes a few sheep would be taken up to the shielings, for their milk made excellent cheese. The boys would drive the other livestock away to the herding grounds. At night they would be herded back again to a fold near the houses for protection against predators.

Next day the dairying would start, cream set aside for churning, milk for the cheese press. The cheese was sometimes smoked. Large quantities of superb butter and cheese were made over the summer. Some would be sent down to the men at home, some would be preserved in kegs buried in the peat. A form of milk shake was made by frothing up a cupful of milk with a special little plunger called a 'fro stick'. A favourite dish was curds, and the whey was drunk. Nothing was wasted. Young and old would bloom with health, so well fed were they in the hill air after the long winter.

Life at the shielings was a busy time but essentially a happy one. Many songs were composed and sung as the work went on. There were love songs too as the herd boys cast eyes at the dairy maids –

Brown-haired girl, I would choose you,
Ho-ro, you would be my choice.
Brown-haired girl, I would choose you
For sweetness and for beauty.
Brown-haired girl of the fold,
Young did I give you my devotion.
No other shall take you from me
Unless he wins you with gold.

Dancing on the green would fill the long summer evenings. Standards of morality were high and mothers were there to act as chaperones and create a family atmosphere. The girls were taught all the dairying skills and also the skills of spinning. Much flax was spun because the light was better in the summer evenings. The thread was fine, and later made into linen.

The women would also gather the lichens and roots they used for dyeing the wool, and herbs used for medicines. Herb lore had been handed down through the generations. Infusions of thyme and heather made health-giving drinks. Bunches of myrtle kept the flies away in the dairy. The boys, who had to spend long days herding the non-milking cattle, would pass the time gathering herbs with the women's guidance, some becoming knowledgeable botanists.

Others would do wood-carving. Just with the aid of a sharp knife, many attractive items could be made – spoons, spirtles, milk-whisks, even coggs for holding milk. The boys would also provide for the larder, with a roe deer surreptitiously shot, a rabbit snared or some trout guddled in the burn. Milk was regarded as a food and a medicine. It had always been so, since the earliest times. Goats' milk was thought to be the best for restoring strength.

While life at the shielings was going happily along, the men back at the crofts were also busily employed and no doubt enjoying many a céilidh together with a smoke and a dram in the evenings. Some would take the opportunity to re-thatch the roofs of their houses. The old thatch, heavily impregnated with peat-fire smoke, would serve as good organic fertiliser and was ploughed into the arable ground in spring.

The men would also do tanning, work in leather and make brogues for the family. Some were skilled weavers and tailors and could get on with this work when there were no family demands on their time.

Towards the end of summer, when the hill grass was getting past its best, there would be a move home from the shielings, with the cattle fat and glossy, some of them ready for the long drive to the autumn markets in the south. The children would be similarly robust and ready for the trials of winter and long days at school. There would be good stocks of butter and cheese and lengths of woollen and linen yarn – the produce of the summer days on the hills.

So there was great rejoicing as the homecoming was celebrated. In good heart, the community was ready to tackle the next big job – the harvest – which meant provision for the people and their precious cattle through the coming winter.

All in all, the sojourn at the shielings was a valuable part of the pattern of the year, beneficial to all concerned, people and beasts alike. Sadly, little trace can now be found of these places that were once so full of life. The small dwellings have weathered away with time, though patches of bright green sward still mark the spots where the cows grazed. And the songs remain –

Brown-haired lass of the shieling,
I would surely sit with you
On the top of the high hills
And on the shieling of the hillocks.

Sung at winter céilidhs, as they still are today, these songs bring back all the memories of the shieling days.

Johnson and Boswell Travel
by Loch Ness

AT THE START of their famous journey to the Hebrides in the autumn of 1773, Dr Samuel Johnson and James Boswell spent their first night in the Highland area at Fort George, the military establishment east of Inverness, where they were liberally entertained by the Governor. On their way next day to Inverness they did not stop to view the site of the battle of Culloden. It is not known if this was a deliberate omission, but it is thought that Johnson was secretly a Jacobite at heart. He certainly deplored the fact that the Gaelic language was beginning to die out, as schoolchildren were deliberately taught in English.

In Inverness they stayed two nights, putting up at Mackenzie's Inn, enjoying the company of several congenial new acquaintances and dining off roasted kid which 'Dr Johnson much relished.'

They then hired horses for themselves, one for their guide Joseph and a fourth to carry their luggage. Two Highlanders – John Hay and Lauchland Vass – accompanied them on foot and were to return the horses when the travellers took ship to the islands.

They must have made a strange-looking equipage. Dr

Johnson was 65, 6 feet tall, stout and stooped. He was short-sighted, slightly deaf and liable to make sudden movements. Because of his weight he had to shift horses from time to time. Boswell described his way of riding thus: 'When he rode he had no command or direction of his horse, but was carried on as if in a balloon.' Though subject to bouts of depression he travelled with enjoyment and showed courtesy to all he met. Boswell was just half his companion's age, short, dark and always busy.

About three miles from the town, making for the road on the south shore of Loch Ness, the 'Wade' road, they stopped to look at the 'Druid's Temple' – a circle of large stones by the road, near Crow Wood. They were not impressed, Dr Johnson observing that 'to see one Druidical temple is only to see that it is nothing, for there is neither art nor power in it and seeing one is quite enough.'

They came to Loch Ness and Boswell said: 'It was a delightful day. Loch Ness and the road upon the side of it, shaded with birch trees and the hills above it, pleased us much.' On hearing that the water in Loch Ness never freezes, Dr Johnson said: 'Lough Ness deserves to be diligently examined.'

They passed through the village of Dores, but made no note of it in their journals. A little further they came to what they called a 'Hut':

It was a wretched little hovel of earth only, I think, and for a window had only a small hole, which was stopped with a piece of turf that was taken out occasionally to let in light. In the middle of the room ... was a fire of peat, the smoke going out a hole in the roof. She had a pot upon it, with goat's flesh, boiling. There was at one end, under the same roof, but divided

by a kind of partition made of wattles, a pen or fold in which
we saw a good many kids.

This is a good description of the houses of the time. The woman
was a little wary of her visitors as in this same place a girl had been
abducted and an old woman strangled by Government soldiers
after the battle of Culloden, some 27 years previously.

She was a Fraser, her husband a forester. With the usual Highland hospitality she offered them a dram. Her only request was for
snuff, her luxury. They had none, but gave her sixpences, tasted
her whisky, and parted 'with many prayers in Erse'. The Gaelic
language was often known as 'Erse' or 'Irish'. Coming to the
hostelry known as the 'General's hut', they dined, and dined
well, on 'mutton-chops, a broiled chicken and bacon and eggs
and a bottle of Malaga.'

Towards evening they came to the river, which makes the
celebrated fall of 'Fiers' (Foyers). Johnson said 'the country...
strikes the imagination with all the gloom and grandeur of
Siberian solitude.' And '... we saw a channel torn, as it seems,
through black piles of stone, by which the stream is obstructed and
broken, till it comes to a very steep descent, of such dreadful
depth, that we were naturally inclined to turn aside our eyes.'
Though they were impressed by the setting, they were not seeing the falls at their most fearsome, as there had been a spell of
drought.

It was late when they arrived at Fort Augustus, having covered
33 miles in the day, which was good going. They were met at the
door by Governor Trapaud, an officer of Huguenot descent, who
had fought at the battle of Culloden, whom Boswell described as
a man of 'excellent animal spirits, the conversation of a soldier,

and somewhat of a Frenchman, to which his extraction entitles him. We passed a very good evening till 12, then went to bed.'

Anne McVicker was at the fort at the time, a young girl of 17. Her father, who had been involved in the war in America, was barrack-master. She later married the young chaplain at the fort and became well known as Anne Grant of Laggan, who wrote the *Letters from the Mountains* and other works. She and her father would have had much to tell the travellers about life in America.

Dr Johnson said: 'It was comfortable to find ourselves in a well built square and a neatly furnished house, in good Company, with a good supper before us: in short with all the conveniences of civilised life in the midst of the rude mountains.' The following day, refusing, regretfully, an invitation to stay to dinner, they made off, by the old military road to upper Glen Moriston, on their way to the west and their adventurous journey to the islands.

They stopped for the night at the inn at Aonach, a small hostelry with rooms lined with wattle. Here they first heard about the Clearances that were taking place as the local laird was raising rents, felling timber and forcing the tenants to move. They were surprised and delighted to find that the daughter of the house had 'the English pronounciation' and could converse fluently. Johnson gave her a book 'which I happened to have about me'. It was a copy of *Cocker's Arithmetic*. In the morning their host saw them on their way, as was the custom, and told them, with pride, how, in former times, Macdonald, Lord of the Isles, would stay at the Inn at Aonach on his travels and would exchange shirts with Macdonald, Aonach, as a sign of loyalty.

After their return they each wrote an account of their tour.

These accounts are among the first and best pieces of travel-writing ever to appear. Their authenticity also makes them valuable historical documents, with the acute observations of two widely read and – in Boswell's case – widely travelled men of letters.

General George Wade

GEORGE WADE was born in 1673 in West Meath, Ireland. His grandfather had been a major in Cromwell's army and had acquired land there. George joined the army as a young ensign of 17 and saw service in many parts of Europe. By 1714 he had risen to the rank of major general and in 1725 he was appointed Commander-in-Chief in Scotland. The government was much concerned about the 'rebellious Scots', particularly since the uprising of 1715. In 1722 Wade had been elected as MP for Bath, a place considered a 'hot-bed of Jacobitism'. It was hoped he would help to quell potential disturbances.

When Wade, as Commander-in-Chief in Scotland, set about his task of trying to establish order in the Highlands, his first concern was to re-organise the 'Highland Companies', units of local militia with Gaelic-speaking officers who were acting as keepers of the peace. Next, his plan was to pass a new Disarming Act, as the present one was largely disregarded, to establish new forts at Kilchumein and Inverness and to repair the barracks at Fort William. He had a vessel of 30 tons built on the lochside – the *Highland Galley*. It could transport 60 soldiers or 20 tons of provisions from Inverness to the fort of Kilchumein, taking 3–4 hours in passage. On her first trip she was 'mightily adorned with colours and fired her guns several times.' She must have been an impressive sight.

In his report on the situation Wade said: 'the Highlands of Scotland are still more impracticable from the want of roads and bridges.' So the building of roads and bridges, primarily to allow the easier passage of troops about the country, was begun.

He soon came to realise the enormity of the task. The country was virtually unmapped, and subject to the destructive forces of heavy falls of snow and of the surging waters of rivers in spate. His labour force was unskilled and work could only be carried on during the summer months. Up to 500 soldiers were employed at a time, with some skilled or semi-skilled civilians. He persuaded the government to increase the rate of pay for men working on the roads and he made sure that their supplies of food were adequate. The work, with pick, spade, shovel, iron crowbar, was extremely hard. It was reckoned that a yard and a half of roadway was all a man could make in a day. He saw to it that 'Beside the plaid clothing to be furnished every two years each soldier was to receive from his Captain a pair of brogues every six weeks, a pair of stockings every three months, a shirt and a cravat every six months.'

His working party consisted of one captain, two subalterns, two sergeants, two corporals, one drummer and 100 men. The men handed in their weapons. They worked a 10-hour day. As bridges took the place of fords more skilled civilians were brought in – masons, wallers, pavers, carpenters. Blacksmiths set up forges for the repair of equipment and the shoeing of horses. 'Reserves', employed on a rotational basis, acted as messengers and letter carriers. One wonders what the local people made of all the activity.

In most places the width of the road was 16 feet. With the foundations dug, large stones broken by gunpowder were lowered into the trench. Smaller stones were smashed by sledgehammer. Then gravel to a depth of two feet was beaten in with shovels and feet. Earth was thrown up into banks on each side with drainage trenches bordering them. An open diagonal cross-drain was also dug. Many traces of Wade's roads remain. One in particular on the southern outskirts of Inverness is now designated a 'footpath' and can be followed for several miles. In places the method of construction can be clearly seen.

When a certain section of road was finished Wade would join his Highwaymen in a feast of roast ox. He managed to persuade the Exchequer to allow them to brew their own beer as this was a healthier drink than the spirits sold to them by the people. It was decided that 'the remote situation of the garrison, the unwholesomeness of the water, the spirits sold by the people of the country, the salt provisions, render it necessary for their health to provide good and wholesome drink. It is necessary to brew beer because of the heavy land carriage.'

They would make camp about every ten miles, usually in small 'huts' made in local style, of turf, with a thatch of heather. Marker stones were placed along the line of the road. One, on the road south from Inverness, now the busy A9, is known as Wade's Stone. It stands at eight feet and had to be moved, with extreme care, from its original place. The date 1729 is carved on it. The story is told that Wade, who was six feet tall, placed a guinea on top of the stone one day. Returning the following year, he found it still there.

Writing from Kilchumein, by that time known as Fort Augustus, in 1727, Wade said:

The great road of communication is so far advanced that I

travelled to Fort William in my coach and six to the great wonder of the country people who had never seen such a machine in these parts before. They ran from their houses close to the coach and, looking up, bowed to the coachman, little regarding us that were within. It is not unlikely that they looked upon him as a sort of Prime Minister that guided so important a machine.

Perhaps the most dramatic of Wade's road-buildings was that of the Corrieyairick, on the original drove road leading from Fort Augustus to Speyside. It rises to over 2,500 feet and, in winter, conditions can be extreme. Many people, on foot or on horseback, have perished on their way. Thirteen traverses lead from the Speyside end to the summit. Going down towards the shieling grounds in a sheltered spot between the hills above Fort Augustus, known as the 'Milky Hollow' or 'Dairy Glade' and subsequently nick-named 'Snugborough' by Wade's men, he gave them an 'oxfeast'. It was 30 October 1732, the King's birthday, but the feast was really to celebrate the completion of the road. Six oxen were roasted!

Wade reported: 'the new road ... is now made as easy and practicable for wheeled carriages as any road in the country.' Anne Grant and her husband drove over it to their new home in Laggan in 1779.

Today the road is a long-distance walk, its devotees enjoying the wildlife and the superb views from the summit. Other 'Wade Roads' make attractive walking in many parts of the Highlands. Some, tarred over and widened, carry the motor traffic of modern times.

At the time of their building they were not universally

approved of. Edmund Burt, the engineer, wrote to a friend in England about the objections to the new roads and bridges:

> Those chiefs and other gentlemen complain that thereby an easy passage is opened into their country for strangers who, in time, by their suggestion of liberty, will destroy or weaken that attachment of their vassals which it is so necessary for them to support and preserve. That, their fastnesses being laid open, they are deprived of that security from invasion which they formerly enjoyed. That the bridges, in particular, will render the ordinary people effeminate. The middle order say the roads are to them an inconvenience, instead of being useful... for their horses never being shod, the gravel would soon whet away their hoofs. The lowest class allege that the gravel is intolerable to their naked feet.

It was not long, however, before Wade was able to report: 'The Highlanders, by the ease and expediency of transporting their merchandise begin to approve and applaud what they at first repined at and submitted to with reluctancy.'

By 1733, 250 miles of road had been engineered. Eventually 40 stone bridges were built. The greatest of these was the bridge over the river Tay at Aberfeldy. It is still in use today, a handsome structure 400 feet long with five arches. Wade was clearly concerned about the future maintenance of the roads and had battles with the Treasury over securing a regular grant for repairs.

Wade's relations with his soldiers were good and those with the people among whom he worked appear to have been cordial. He was keen to see that provision for the education of children should be made. A school set up at Fort Augustus by the SSPCK had had to be closed as the teaching was in English and the children only understood Gaelic. As a soldier who had become an engineer and then an administrator, he had been made aware of the many social problems of the area. His time there, he would say later, included the happiest days of his life.

Then, in 1740, he left the Highlands, and three years later, promoted Field Marshal, he returned to soldiering. At the age of 72, after a period of ill health, he was back in England and marching north to put down the Jacobite uprising of 1745. At this time an extra verse was added to the National Anthem:

> God grant that Marshall Wade
> May by thy mighty aid
> Victory bring.
> May he sedition hush
> And like a torrent rush
> Rebellious Scots to crush.
> God save the King!

Wade's last command was not a successful one. At the age of 75 he died, leaving money for a monument to himself in Westminster Abbey.

Though not as successful as he had hoped in suppressing rebellion in the Highlands, his perception that the lack of communication in the area was the greatest obstacle to the pursuit of peace, and his tremendous efforts to overcome that obstacle, have secured him a place as a pioneer in the modernisation of the country.

His successor as a road-builder, who had become Inspector of Roads, was William Caulfield, a fellow Irishman. They had worked together for many years. He remained in charge of the military roads until his death in 1767. It was Caulfield who composed the famous lines:

> If you'd seen these roads before they were made
> You would lift up your hands and bless General Wade.

They were inscribed on an obelisk that formerly stood on the side of the road between Inverness and Inverary.

As the value of better communication – Wade's legacy – came to be fully realised, some minor roads were made, with sub-tenants liable for six days' labour each year. Quite old men were employed breaking stones by the roadside. In 1803 the Commission for Highland Roads and Bridges was set up, with half the cost of road building to be met by the Government, half by the landowners. These roads were known as Parliamentary roads. Surfaced in modern style, many of them are in use still.

The old Wade Roads are those which give most pleasure to the walker today, crossing wild upland country, lingering by the shores of lochs, bridges great and small delighting the eye. Wade and his Highwaymen have left us this legacy to treasure.

Envoi

ON LOCH NESS today craft still ride the waters – tiny kayaks so fragile that it seems the next grey wave must engulf them; huge floating hotels running cruises to the west coast and the islands; small daily cruise boats; yachts, white or red-sailed; plastic racers; other motor vessels of all kinds. Events are organised. There are regattas and 'raids'. Water skiers practise in one sheltered bay.

The shipping for which the canal was intended – trawlers, commercial vessels, a naval launch or two – rarely uses the waterway now. The little piers where the steamers came to load and unload their cargoes – people, mail, cattle, potatoes – bringing bustle to the settlements along the shore, at Abriachan, Inverfarigaig and other places, have fallen into disrepair. Traffic now moves noisily, on wheels, on tarred and sometimes treacherous lochside roads. Holiday-makers crowd the lay-bys, stopping to stand and stare in the ever-present hope of seeing some strange creature emerge from the depths, of capturing its image in binoculars and camera.

Wildlife of a less spectacular kind, though shy and elusive, can be glimpsed by treading softly, as the Reverend Angus MacFarlane did, on the old tracks by the shore. Otter, fox, pine-marten, squirrel, heron and merganser, the dipper, the redstart and the wren, these and many more would have been the familiars of the early people, moving about in their dug-out canoes, of Deirdre and her lover in the little fort.

This Loch Ness country has been the backdrop to scenes of anguish and of mercy over many centuries. There have been drownings, most often of the unwary, for the big loch is always restive, even under calm.

The Druids, once ruling in the sombre oak groves, were superseded by Columba and his followers, who brought Christianity this way, travelling in their frail curraghs, and carrying their message of redemption. The scars of feuds and of wars, ancient and modern, are here. Cromwell sailed his frigate and Cumberland brought his Redcoats to threaten the 'wild' men of the glens. Galleys ferried provisions to the garrisoned army at Fort Augustus. These events live on in long memories. But the legacy of the 'good Sir James' remains a practicality in the little, bright green, well-limed fields of the farms he created.

The sweated labour of Wade's Highwaymen and of Telford's navvies brought contact with a wider world and the impact of industrialisation has been felt and accommodated. Further measures in the ceaseless quest for energy may be on the way. There may be more scars to come. But nature is a great healer. Birch and rowan need only a crevice in the rock to find succour for their roots. Banks of primroses crowd the lichen and carpet the moss. Scant soil brings the heather to bloom. Now the osprey is fishing and red kite scythe the sky. Miracles are part of the structure of Telford's 'remarkable valley'.

Bibliography

Adamnan. *Life of Saint Columba*, ed. W. Reeves, Edmonston & Douglas, Edinburgh, 1874

Barron, E.M. *The Scottish Wars of Independence*, Robert Carruthers, Inverness, 1934

Barron, James. *The Northern Highlands in the 19th Century*, 3 vols, 1903-1914, Robert Carruthers, Inverness, 1903

Blaeu, Joannis. *Maps of Britain,* Amsterdam, 1653

Blake, Ian. *Poetry of Scotland*, Diehard, Edinburgh, 2001

Boswell, James. *Journal of a Tour to the Hebrides*, Herneman, London, 1936

Burt, Edmund. *Burt's Letters from the North of Scotland*, Birlinn, Edinburgh, 1998

Cameron, A.D. *The Caledonian Canal,* Canongate Academics, Edinburgh, 1994

Carmichael, Alexander. *Carmina Gadelica*, Scottish Academic Press, Edinburgh, 1976

Ellis, Peter Beresford. *The Ancient World of the Celts*, Constable, London, 1998

Forsyth, R. *Beauties of Scotland,* Grose, Verner and Hood, London, 1808

Fraser, James. *Genealogy of the Frasers 916–1674*, Constable, Edinburgh, 1905

Grant, Anne. *Letters from the Mountains*, Longman, London, 1806

Haldane, A.R.B. *New Ways through the Glens*, Thomas Nelson, London, 1962

The Drove Roads of Scotland, David and Charles, Newton Abbot, 1973

Hutchison, Roger. *Aleister Crowley: The Beast Demystified*, Mainstream, Edinburgh, 1998

Inverness Courier, 1817–2005

Inverness Journal, 1807–1848

Macdonald, Alexander. *Song and Story from Loch Ness-side*, Northern Counties Publishing Co., Inverness, 1914

Mackay, William. *Urquhart and Glenmoriston*, Northern Counties Publishing Co., Inverness, 1893

MacKintosh, Charles Fraser. *Antiquarian Notes*, A & W Mackenzie, Inverness, 1897

Maclennan, Hugh Dan. *Foyers*, Kessock Communications, Inverness, 1996

Martin, Martin. *A Description of the Western Islands of Scotland, Circa 1695*, Birlinn, Edinburgh, 1999

Melville, M.L. *The Story of the Lovat Scouts 1900–1980*, St Andrews Press, Edinburgh, 1981

Name Book, Ordnance Survey, 1871

New Statistical Account of Scotland, 1831, Scottish Academic Press, Edinburgh, reprinted 1985

Pennant, Thomas. *A Tour in Scotland and Voyage to the Hebrides*, 1722, Birlinn, Edinburgh, 1998

Piggott, Stuart. *Scotland before History*, Edinburgh University Press, Edinburgh, 1982

Proceedings of the Society of Antiquaries of Scotland, Vol XXXVI, Neill and Co., Edinburgh, 1902

Queen Victoria. *More Leaves from the Journal of a Life in the Highlands*, Smith, Elderd and Co., London, 1884

Rolt, L.T.C. *Thomas Telford*, Longman, London, 1958

Salmond, J.B. *Wade in Scotland*, Moray Press, Edinburgh and London, 1934

Scottish Society for the Propagation of Christian Knowledge (SSPCK) Schoolmasters 1709–1872, Scottish Record Society, Edinburgh, 1997

Squire, Charles. *Celtic Myths and Legends*, Parragon, Bristol, 1998

Stewart, Colonel David, of Garth, *Sketches of the Highlanders*, Constable and Co., Edinburgh, 1822

Swire, Otta F. *The Highlands and their Legends*, Oliver and Boyd, Edinburgh, 1963

Taylor, Sue Jane and Catriona Murray. '*Bho Dhrobhadh Gaidhealach gu Fasaichean Astrailia*: From Highland Drove to the Australian Outback', *Stornoway Gazette*, 1998

Transactions of the Gaelic Society of Inverness, Inverness, 1871–2005

Transactions of the Inverness Field Club, Inverness, 1875–1925

Wallace, William. *Life and Works of Robert Burns*, Vol 2, ed. R. Chambers, Chambers, Edinburgh, 1896

Wood, Karen. *The Folklore of South Loch Ness-side*, privately published, 1995

Wordsworth, Dorothy. *Recollections of a Tour made in Scotland*, Yale University Press, London, 1997

Chronology

c. 4000 BC	Bronze Age
	First settlers
c. 700 BC to 500 AD	Iron Age
43 AD to 450 AD	Roman occupation of Scotland
142–143	Antonine Wall built
565	St Columba arrives from Ireland
late 6th century	First reported sighting of a monster in the loch
c. 800	Norse invasions
1266	Treaty of Perth ends Norse occupation
1286–1371	Scottish Wars of Independence
1295	'Auld Alliance' established between France and Scotland
1314	Battle of Bannockburn
1513	Battle of Flodden
1603	Union of Scottish and English Crowns
1650s	Cromwell's forces are in the Highlands
1689	Battle of Killiecrankie
1692	Massacre at Glencoe
1707	Union of Parliaments
1715 and 1719	Jacobite uprisings in the Highlands
1724	General George Wade arrives in the Highlands

1745	Jacobite uprising in the Highlands
1746	Battle of Culloden
	Disarming Act
1756	Start of the Seven Years' War in North America
1757	78th Fraser's Highlanders regiment raised
1760	Grant Highlanders regiment raised
1775–1783	American War of Independence
1789	French Revolution
1793–1815	Napoleonic Wars
18th and 19th centuries	Emigration from the Highlands
1801	Thomas Telford in the Highlands
1803	Building started on Caledonian Canal
1822	Caledonian Canal opened
1843	Disruption in the Church of Scotland
1870	Ordnance Survey maps first published
1872	Education Act
1886	Crofters Act
1896	Aluminium works set up at Foyers
1899	Boer War
1914–1918	First World War
1939–1945	Second World War
1960	'Monster Watch' established
1991	37 Tall Ships sail Loch Ness
1998	Abriachan Forest Trust established
2004	Start of new hydroelectric scheme at Glendoe on the east end of Loch Ness

Glossary

céilidh   gathering for talk and music

clarsach   small harp

coronach   lament for the dead

curragh   small round boat made of hide

kelp   a type of seaweed

kelpie   magic water-horse

Index

Some other books published by **LUATH** PRESS

Women of the Highlands

Katharine Stewart

ISBN 1 905222 74 2 HBK £14.99

The Highlands and Islands of Scotland are an evocative and mysterious land, cut off from the rest of Scotland by seas and mountains and developing almost as a separate country for hundreds of years. Epitomising the 'sublime' in philosophical thought of the 18th century, they have been a source of inspiration for poets and writers of all descriptions.

Katharine Stewart takes us to the heart of Highland romance in her history of the women who shaped the land and handed down the legends that have provided such a rich vein of material for generations. From the women of the shielings to ladies at court, from bards to conservationists, authors to folk-singers, *Women of the Highlands* examines how the culture of the Highlands was created and passed down through the centuries, and how the tradition is continuing today.

When was the last witch burnt in the Highlands and what was her crime?

Which Jacobite lady led men to war while her Hanoverian husband stayed at home?

Who were the first Highland women to be recorded in history and what did they do?

And how have women's lives changed since medieval times?

Katharine Stewart recounts the lives and legends of famous Highland and Island women, from Elizabeth Grant of Rothiemurchus to Jane Maxwell, Duchess of Gordon. However, the true essence of the book lies in the abiding sense of the thousands of Highlanders throughout the ages who, though they lived under different laws and in far-off times, have together created the history and culture that produced the Highland women of today.

Katharine Stewart's latest book has the authority of being part of the living tradition it describes.

MARGARET ELPHINSTONE

Writing in the Sand

Angus Dunn

ISBN 1 905222 47 5 PBK £12.99

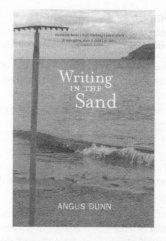

The future hangs on the fall of the sand grains.
And time is running out...

On the tip of the Dark Isle lies the tranquil fishing village of Cromness, where the normal round of domino matches, meetings of the Ladies' guild and twice-daily netting of salmon continues as it always has done. But all is not well.

Down on the beach, an old man rakes the sand, looking for clues to the future. The patterns show him the harmony of the universe, but they also show that there is something wrong in Cromness. Strange things are beginning to happen.

Because this is no ordinary island. Centuries ago, so it is said, the Celtic gods and goddesses took refuge here. Now, behind the walls of the world, there are restless stirring sounds.

Mist descends. Strange animals move through the fog, turnip fields disappear and the fishing fleet begin to blockade the island. As the islanders prepare to celebrate the famed Dark Isle Show, the moment of Truth approaches.

Soon everyone is drawn into the struggle against the shadows that threaten the Dark Isle. But is anyone truly aware of the scale of events? And who will prevail?

It is a latter day baggy monster of a novel... a hallucinogenic soap... the humour at first has shades of Last of the Summer Wine, *alternating with the Goons before going all out for the Monty Python meets James Bond, and don't-scrimp-on-the-turbo-charger method... You'll have gathered by now that this book is a grand read. It's an entertainment. It alternates between compassionate and skilful observations, elegantly expressed and rollercoaster abandonment to a mad narrative.*

NORTHWORDS NOW

A bold, confident debut, packed to the gunnels with memorable characters and wry humour.

THE LIST

A cross between High Road and Dr Who, with a hefty dose of League of Gentlemen thrown in for surreal good measure. It's also funny, imaginative, thrilling and charming, with a colourful cast of unforgettable characters and a page-turning plot that had me gripped to the very last page.

PRESS AND JOURNAL

The Highland Clearances Trail

Rob Gibson

ISBN 1 905222 10 6 PBK £5.99

It is obvious there is a need for an investigation into the nature and scale of the Clearances. The facts have always been subject to revision, but now Rob Gibson's *The Highland Clearances Trail* systematically documents dates, places, names and numbers and in doing so nails the lie that the Clearances were somehow a benevolent act by paternalistic landowners.

Answers the where, why, what and whens of the Highland Clearances and provides an alternative route around the Highlands that will leave the reader with a deeper understanding of this sublime landscape.

It is important to get the whole movement into perspective and examine the truth of the matter and I hope that this well-written book will address the balance.

HIGHLAND NEWS

The Highland Geology Trail

John L. Roberts

ISBN 0 946487 36 7 PBK £5.99

Where can you find the oldest rocks in Europe?

Where can you see ancient hills around 800 million years old?

How do you tell whether a valley was carved out by a glacier, not by a river?

What are the Focoid Beds?

Where do you find rocks folded like putty?

How did the great masses of rock pile up like snow in front of a snowplough?

When did volcanoes spew lava and ash to form Skye, Mull and Rum?

Where can you find fossils on Skye?

This journey of geological discovery through the diverse landforms of the north and west Highlands of Scotland offers the answers to these and many other questions of interest to visitors and local residents alike.

The Hydro Boys

Emma Wood

ISBN 1 84282 047 8 PBK £8.99

The hydro-electric project was a crusade, with a marvellous goal: the prize of affordable power for all from Scottish rainfall.

This book is a journey through time, and across and beneath the Highland landscape... it is not just a story of technology and politics but of people.

I heard about drowned farms and hamlets, the ruination of the salmon-fishing and how Inverness might be washed away if the dams failed inland. I was told about the huge veins of crystal they found when they were tunnelling deep under the mountains and when I wanted to know who 'they' were: what stories I got in reply! I heard about Poles, Czechs, poverty-stricken Irish, German spies, intrepid locals and the heavy drinking, fighting and gambling which went on in the NoSHEB contractors' camps.

EMMA WOOD

Nobody should forget the human sacrifice made by those who built the dams all those years ago. The politicians, engineers and navvies of the era bequeathed to us the major source of renewable energy down to the present day. Their legacy will continue to serve us far into the 21st century.

BRIAN WILSON MP, Energy Minister, THE SCOTSMAN

100 Favourite Scottish Poems

Edited by Stewart Conn

ISBN 1 905222 61 0 PBK £7.99

Poems to make you laugh. Poems to make you cry. Poems to make you think. Poems to savour. Poems to read out loud. To read again, and again. Scottish poems. Old favourites. New favourites – 100 of the best.

Scotland has a long history of producing outstanding poetry. From the humblest but-and-ben to the grandest castle, the nation has a great tradition of celebration and commemoration through poetry. *100 Favourite Scottish Poems* – incorporating the nation's best-loved poems as selected in a BBC Radio Scotland listeners' poll – ranges from the ballads to Burns, from 'Proud Maisie' to 'The Queen of Sheba', and from 'Cuddle Doon' to 'The Jeelie Piece Song'.

Edited by Stewart Conn, poet and first recipient of the Institute of Contemporary Scotland's Iain Crichton Smith Award for services to literature (2006).

... a highly varied collection and one that should fulfill Conn's hopes of whetting the reader's appetite... this is both a taster and a volume of substance.
THE HERALD

Both wit and wisdom, and that fusion of the two which can touch the heart as well as the mind, distinguishes the work selected by Stewart Conn [in] this lovely little book.

Robert Nye, THE SCOTSMAN

Luath Press Limited
committed to publishing well written books worth reading

LUATH PRESS takes its name from Robert Burns, whose little collie Luath (*Gael.*, swift or nimble) tripped up Jean Armour at a wedding and gave him the chance to speak to the woman who was to be his wife and the abiding love of his life. Burns called one of 'The Twa Dogs' Luath after Cuchullin's hunting dog in *Ossian's Fingal*. Luath Press was established in 1981 in the heart of Burns country, and is now based a few steps up the road from Burns' first lodgings on Edinburgh's Royal Mile.

Luath offers you distinctive writing with a hint of unexpected pleasures.

Most bookshops in the UK, the US, Canada, Australia, New Zealand and parts of Europe either carry our books in stock or can order them for you. To order direct from us, please send a £sterling cheque, postal order, international money order or your credit card details (number, address of cardholder and expiry date) to us at the address below. Please add post and packing as follows: UK – £1.00 per delivery address; overseas surface mail – £2.50 per delivery address; overseas airmail – £3.50 for the first book to each delivery address, plus £1.00 for each additional book by airmail to the same address. If your order is a gift, we will happily enclose your card or message at no extra charge.

Luath Press Limited
543/2 Castlehill
The Royal Mile
Edinburgh EH1 2ND
Scotland
Telephone: 0131 225 4326 (24 hours)
Fax: 0131 225 4324
email: sales@luath.co.uk
Website: www.luath.co.uk